C000124632

IMAGES OF ENGLAND

WELLINGTON
IN THE 1940S AND '50S

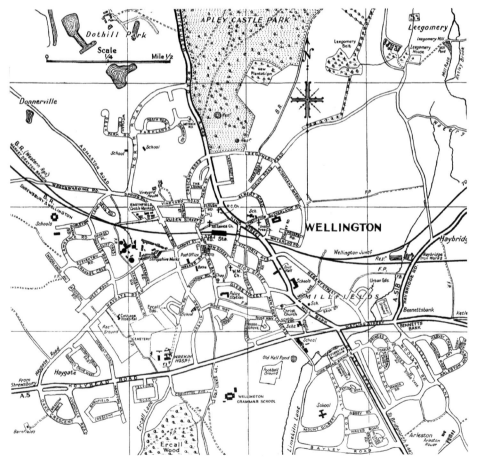

IMAGES OF ENGLAND

WELLINGTON

IN THE 1940S AND '50S

ALLAN FROST

TEMPUS

For my brother, David.

Frontispiece: The Wellington coat of arms was granted to the town in 1951 by the College of Arms after much research by the former Clerk to the Urban Council, John S. Broad; John Broad Avenue is named after him. The design of the coat of arms includes a castle (a reference to Apley Castle), two fleurs-de-lys (from the arms of France which were quartered in the royal arms of Charles I), a lion rampant (from the arms of the Charltons of Apley Castle), a fret (from the arms of Eyton and Cludde) and a bugle horn (from the arms of Lord Forester). The portcullis is another reference to Apley Castle.

The map is a town plan of Wellington in 1958.

First published 2006

Tempus Publishing Limited
The Mill, Brimscombe Port,
Stroud, Gloucestershire, GL5 2QG
www.tempus-publishing.com

© Allan Frost, 2006

The right of Allan Frost to be identified as the Author
of this work has been asserted in accordance with the
Copyrights, Designs and Patents Act 1988.

All rights reserved. No part of this book may be reprinted
or reproduced or utilised in any form or by any electronic,
mechanical or other means, now known or hereafter invented,
including photocopying and recording, or in any information
storage or retrieval system, without the permission in writing
from the Publishers.

British Library Cataloguing in Publication Data.
A catalogue record for this book is available from the British Library.

ISBN 0 7524 3767 4

Typesetting and origination by Tempus Publishing Limited.
Printed in Great Britain.

Contents

Acknowledgements

Many people and organisations have contributed information and illustrations for this book, including Abbey Color, author's collection, J. Addison, B. Bagnall, N. Ball, Barbers, D. Beechey, J. Bradburn, K. Burke, J. and M. Butler, J. Croft, D. Cross, H. Davies, J. Fray, D. Edwards, M. Edwards, G. Evans, B. and C. Felton, D. Frost, P. Frost, M. Greatholder, V. Harrison, V. Hordley, K. Hitchin, D. Houlston, M. Hullin, P. Impson, Ironbridge Gorge Museum, F. Jones, P. Jones, J. Lewis, M. Machin, P. Marston, M. McCrea, E. Moody, A. Morris, B. Morris, C. and W. Newbold, I. Nicholls, R. Nicholls, B. Parker, G. Passant, N. Pitchford, R. Poulter, C. Pye, P. Reade, Shrewsbury Records and Research Library, *Shropshire Star*, I. Skelton, G. Smith, R. Sterling, *Telford Journal*, D. Treherne, M. Ward, *Wellington Journal & Shrewsbury News*, Wellington Library, *Wellington News*, J. Whittingham, P. Williams and Woolworths.

I am very grateful to them all, as well as for the help and support given by my long-suffering wife Dorothy, and apologise sincerely to anyone who has been inadvertently omitted. Every effort has been made to correctly identify the events and people portrayed in the illustrations.

A view of Wellington in 1958, looking north-east from the Ercall Hill. Christ Church can be seen (centre right), as can Wrekin College (centre left). A deep cutting through the wooded slopes of the Ercall Hill (foreground) now accommodates the M54 motorway. The photograph emphasises the fact that at that time Wellington was still essentially a market town surrounded by farmland.

Introduction

This is the prequel to my book *Wellington in 1960*; its evocative and nostalgic photographs and commentary touched a nerve with Wellingtonians past and present. There's something about the town which creates strong feelings of affection and loyalty, perhaps more so since the development of the Telford conurbation in recent years. People need a sense of belonging, not to a vast expanse of modern development but rather to a traditional settlement with its own distinctive character.

Perhaps that's why *Wellington in 1960* and, indeed, other local histories have become so popular in recent years. They record events of years gone by, when there was a greater sense of community spirit. Standards of life may not have been so advanced but, in spite of all the hardships, people tended to work together for the common good and, as a result, created close bonds of friendship with their neighbours.

It didn't matter in which part of the town you lived. There were, of course, 'natural' social divisions and the view someone had of you could be influenced by the street in which you lived. This became increasingly noticeable during the period covered by this book simply because of the creation of large council housing estates, such as those west of the former gasworks and on both sides of Dawley Road. These stood out from middle-class streets like Herbert Avenue and Victoria Avenue, which were themselves cast into shadow by those who could afford to live along Waterloo Road or certain parts of Holyhead Road.

Wellington's folk loved their town. This was probably never more apparent than during the years of the Second World War, when the trials, tribulations, restrictions and privations suffered by a country threatened with invasion and German domination resulted in a radical change to society's attitudes.

Everyone, from whatever walk of life, struggles to make a living. Standards, however high or low, inevitably fall during a war yet there is something in the British character that enables us to cope with each and every setback. Wellington contributed its fair share to the war effort.

Allied forces may have won the war but the social consequences were far-reaching. Nothing could be the same again. Hostilities ended in 1945 but another ten years would pass before rationing ended and some sense of normality returned.

Encouraged by successive governments to breathe new life into Britain's towns, local councils embarked on ambitious projects to improve the quality of life for people who had made so many sacrifices. Wellington Urban and Rural District Councils seized the opportunity and began to change the look of the town and its district, not always for the good. However, from the social point of view, the extreme poverty of the 1930s would eventually be eradicated.

In 1959, the concept of Telford was absent from everyone's mind. Wellington was still the dominant centre of commerce and entertainment in east Shropshire and had every reason to expect the situation to continue. Thriving during the week and almost silent on Sundays and after early closing on Wednesday afternoons, the town was gradually recovering from the war and its after-effects.

This book reveals what happened, how Wellington coped and what it did to regenerate itself. For those who were there at the time, I hope it brings back some happy memories and revives others that should never be forgotten.

If you weren't there, read on and discover an important period in Wellington's past.

Allan Frost
December 2005

One of the last sheep sales at Wellington Smithfield, c. 1940. The Ministry of Food suspended livestock auctions for over ten years to guarantee meat supplies to besieged Britons both during and after the war.

Children did their bit to help the war effort. This group of 'scavengers' stand outside the Wellington Rural District Council offices in Tan Bank before scouring all parts of the town for recyclable rubbish, which would ultimately be used in the manufacture of ships to replace those lost at sea.

one

Coping
with War

In 1940 the Second World War, although just a few months old, was well under way. People were already suffering. It was gradually dawning on them that it would be a long, drawn-out affair requiring considerable patience, courage and resilience. Food, clothing and petrol rationing had been introduced in response to attacks on ships bringing supplies from Commonwealth and other countries. Britain was becoming more and more isolated; it was obvious that belts needed to be tightened and extra efforts made to supplement an already reduced food supply.

The Ministry of Food suspended auctions at and took control over Wellington Smithfield: it became a Certification Centre for grading and distribution of livestock in the area. Farmers struggled to increase the supply of crops, making considerable use of female labour (the Land Army) to compensate for absent men who had joined the armed forces. As the war progressed, German and Italian prisoners of war held in nearby camps (such as those at Hadley) supplemented the depleted farming workforce.

On the domestic front, households were encouraged to 'Dig for Victory' by cultivating their gardens to grow more vegetables. A few even kept pigs and chickens, providing a welcome addition to the family's meagre diet despite the fact that keeping such creatures inevitably led to an increase in rats and other vermin. The council also provided allotments, including those in the grounds of what is now New College (prior to 1940 it had been the Girls' and Boys' High School) and alongside the alleyway from Golf Links Lane to Roseway. A few folk dabbled in poaching. It was a period of severe austerity when even the better off had to make do as best they could.

Newspapers, including the *Wellington Journal & Shrewsbury News*, provided valuable information on how to cook using minimal ingredients. 'Siren tea', so-called because the leaves barely had time to get wet, let alone infuse, so that the liquid was almost 'all-clear' as signalled by an air-raid siren, is just one example of how humour helped in a time of adversity. Butter rations were so small that lard or beef dripping acted as substitutes. Novel ways were devised to serve up leftovers that would hitherto have been thrown away or fed to pigs. Desperate times called for desperate measures. Tasteless food was better than hunger.

Food shops were strictly regulated to ensure that no provisions were wasted and, as far as possible, no one had more than their fair share of the country's limited and diminishing resources. The author's grandmother, Mary Jane Frost, owned a bakery and grocery shop in New Street and often found herself giving away some of her own family's rations so that customers received no less than their entitlement. Other shopkeepers were not so generous. Fruit from overseas became a rarity, so much so that once news spread that bananas or oranges were on sale at a particular greengrocer's, a crowd of hopefuls appeared from nowhere, desperate to buy at least one, whatever the price, to share with their relatives.

As the war continued, so did its impact on the people. The *Wellington Journal & Shrewsbury News* played an important role in informing its readers about many war-related topics, including how ration books could be obtained. It also tried to boost morale by printing photographs of 'our boys' in uniform and the enormous number of weddings which took place during periods of leave.

Opposite above: The Wrekin Beacon, 1958. It was erected during the early 1940s to warn friendly aircraft away from the summit of The Wrekin Hill. It was operated remotely from RAF Shawbury.

Opposite below: Air-raid wardens conduct exercises with civilian volunteers in the streets of Wellington, July 1941. Such events provided vital experience to all concerned should the town be attacked by enemy aircraft.

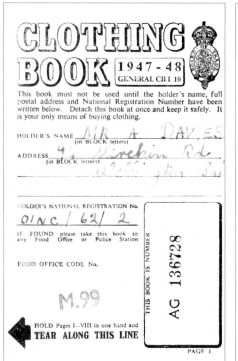

CLOTHING BOOK 1947-48
GENERAL CB1 10

This book must not be used until the holder's name, full postal address and National Registration Number have been written below. Detach this book at once and keep it safely. It is your only means of buying clothing.

HOLDER'S NAME (in BLOCK letters) MR A DAVIES

ADDRESS (in BLOCK letters)

HOLDER'S NATIONAL REGISTRATION No.
OINC / 62/ 2
IF FOUND please take this book to any Food Office or Police Station

FOOD OFFICE CODE No.
M.99

THIS BOOK IS NUMBER
AG 136728

HOLD Pages I—VIII in one hand and
TEAR ALONG THIS LINE

PAGE I

THIS
CERTIFICATE OF HONOUR
IS AWARDED TO
WELLINGS, REGENT ST.
SAVINGS GROUP
IN RECOGNITION OF SPECIAL ACHIEVEMENT
DURING THE
WINGS FOR VICTORY
NATIONAL SAVINGS CAMPAIGN 1943

I EXTEND MY THANKS TO ALL CONCERNED IN THIS IMPORTANT NATIONAL SERVICE.

Archibald Sinclair
SECRETARY OF STATE FOR AIR

Above left: Ration books dictated what could be bought.

Above right: Businesses supported the war effort in many ways.

All motor vehicles, like this railway goods yard lorry seen here in 1941, were required to fit slitted caps on their headlights to limit the amount of light shed during night-time driving. The outer wheel arches were also painted white for visibility. Petrol supplies were strictly rationed.

two

The War
Effort

Many men, some of them under age, volunteered to join the forces as soon as war began but not in sufficient quantities to sustain operational needs. Conscription followed and, unless there was a good reason for not being accepted, call-up notices were met with some trepidation. Memories and horrific tales of the First World War were still fresh in some people's minds but there was little chance of avoiding service. The country had to be defended. Consequently, men with no experience found themselves thrust into the front line. They suffered terribly. However, it is not within the scope of this book to recount their tales of heroism.

There were a few conscientious objectors, people whose beliefs would not permit them to bear arms against a fellow human. One such was Mr Scott, who ran a jewellery shop in Market Square. He was arrested and ordered by the court to spend time each week doing clerical work for the war effort.

Other people were exempt from military service because they worked in 'reserved occupations'. The author's father, Leslie Frost, fell into this category. He was a draughtsman at Sankey's engineering works in Hadley and designed, among other things, components for Spitfire aircraft. During his spare time he was in the Home Guard and became munitions and weapons training officer for his local platoon, a fact which may account for several rifle shells, hand grenades, firing pins and a smoke bomb being discovered in his attic after his death in 1984. He liked to take his work home.

Following hastily devised guidelines, townsfolk did all they could to support the government and prepared to defend themselves against the possibility of attack. Blackout notices were posted around the town and local garages did a brief but roaring trade in adapting vehicle headlamps to limit the amount of light emitted at night. Most households fitted thick material or boards over their windows, and homes with electricity used low-glow bulbs to reduce the likelihood of being fined if light were visible from outside at night. Air-raid wardens roamed the streets at night to check no lights could be seen. These precautions were essential to reduce the possibility of enemy aircraft seeing settlements during their night flights over the area.

Even road signs pointing to other towns and villages were removed to hinder enemy movement in case of invasion, and local businesses, such as Wellington Laundry off Prince's Street, appointed someone to act as fire-watcher in case of attack. (Amusing detail is given in the author's book *The Wellington Sanitary Steam Laundry*.) The council oversaw the creation of air-raid shelters dotted around the town; there were a couple along Mill Lane and adjacent to the allotments in the grounds of what is now New College. Another was situated near the bus shelters on the present Parade car park.

Wellington was not in the front line but its people suffered in different ways. The *Wellington Journal & Shrewsbury News* gave regular reports of those killed, missing and taken prisoner but was unable, because of censorship, to give many details of how the war was progressing; that sort of information was reported, under severe restriction and censorship, via radio and the national press.

In addition to forming several platoons of the Home Guard (one of which was based at the Drill Hall in King Street), local residents were called upon to take part in training exercises to learn how to cope with casualties. They were also required, if they had a spare room, to provide accommodation (billets) for folk arriving in ever-increasing numbers to work at the newly-constructed Civilian Ordnance Depot at nearby Donnington. Anyone objecting, for whatever reason, could find themselves arrested: there were a few instances of married women whose husbands were serving abroad not wanting to comply because of the scandal that was bound to arise by having an unrelated male lodger.

There were several campaigns conducted to aid the war effort. Children scoured the town collecting paper, tins, saucepans and anything else that could be recycled. Events, like garden parties, took place to raise money to build aircraft for the RAF or ships for the Navy. Virtually every inch of metal fence in the town was removed, including the gates outside New Street Methodist church and the Chad Valley Wrekin toy factory, as well as railings embedded in garden and school walls.

Right: Home on leave before embarking for service in North Africa and the Italian Campaign, Private Reg Dunn from Haygate Road gets to know his new young nephew, Michael Greatholder. Reg, aged twenty, volunteered for the 3rd Battalion of the Grenadier Guards. He was wounded in the assault on Monte Casino and invalided back to England; he spent time recovering at the convalescent hospital at Orleton Hall in 1944. Before the war, Reg worked as a turner at R. Groom & Son's timber yard. Michael Greatholder eventually became editor of the *Telford Journal.*

Below: Home Guard Signallers, 1943. Note the crash-helmeted motorcycle despatch rider on the right.

THE BRITISH BROADCASTING CORPORATION
Broadcasting House, London, W.1
Telephone: Welbeck 4468   Telegrams: Broadcasts, Telex, London
Date as postmark

REFERENCE: 28/KH

The B.B.C. has pleasure in informing you that a message of greetings to you from   **India** will be broadcast in the General Forces Prog. at   9.30 a.m.   on Sunday, 15th July

P/52/D

The BBC made good use of its international radio network by enabling service personnel posted abroad to send messages to their families back home. It was a tremendous morale-booster.

Specially printed lightweight paper enabled soldiers to send personal notes from exotic countries like India to the folks back home.

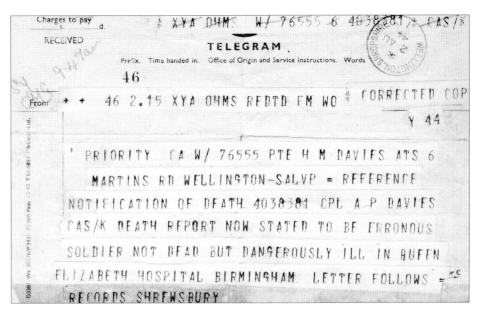

The delivery of a telegram usually meant grief. It is impossible to imagine the trauma suffered by Hilda, Percy Davies' wife, when she received two telegrams stating that her husband had been killed in action. The telegram above was delivered a few days later. Percy survived the war and became a well-known figure at Wellington Smithfield and Wellington market.

Frank Bowles (marked with a cross), a former pupil at Wellington Grammar School for Boys, worked for the Post Office until joining the Royal Naval Volunteer Reserve in 1940. He became a pilot in the Fleet Air Arm, serving on HMS *Victorious*. He lost his life while flying a Barracuda torpedo bomber during an attack on German battleship *Tirpitz* in Alten Fjord, Norway, on 4 April 1944.

They Found Wellington Doll In Greece

TO be reminded of home is probably one of the happiest experiences that comes to men serving their country abroad Here, shortly, is the story of two local men . . . their names are Norman Upton (L.A.C.), of Red Lake, near Wellington and Ernest Butler, of Broseley.

Ever since they left England they have been together and have seen service in Greece, Crete and Iraq, being with the R.A.F. in the Middle East. When Upton, Butler and another friend (Reg. Dyke) were leaving Greece, they found on the beach—a doll! And to their astonishment they found on it the name "Norah Wellings, Wellington."

Upton's father (Mr. W. Upton), who has just heard this story in a letter from his son, says the three have since carried the doll with them as a mascot. You can see it in the picture, Upton holding it, with Butler on his left and Dyke on his right. Incidentally Butler used to be employed by Dr. Prentice, of Wellington

Left: In spite of strict censorship by the government, local newspapers like the *Wellington Journal & Shrewsbury News* did their utmost to bring newsworthy items to their pages. Paper supplies were greatly diminished during the war years but newspapers were essential to let people know at least something about what was happening on various fronts. As well as reporting happier events, especially weddings, it also notified readers of local servicemen and women captured, killed or missing in action. This article describes how a doll made at Norah Wellings' toy factory in Wellington was discovered by local lads serving in Greece in August 1941. No one ever found out how the doll came to be washed up on a beach.

Below: Norah Wellings' internationally famous toy factory in the former King Street Baptist chapel underwent considerable expansion from the 1920s until it closed at the end of the 1950s.

Right: The letter of thanks sent by King George VI to schoolchildren throughout the country to help them understand the sacrifices and commitment made by so many citizens during the war. One of the intentions of the letter was to make children proud to be British and feel part of a free nation.

Below: Air-Raid Precautions, Casualty Section, 1945. Back row, fourth from left: Audrey Smith. Middle row, second from left: Violet York. Middle row, third from right: Muriel Bishop. Middle row, second from right: Edna Dunn. Front row, third from left: Mr Jones. Front row, centre: Dr W.R.H. Pooler. Front row, third from right: Mr Ferriday. Front row, extreme right: Dorothy Jones(?). Other members include J.M. Blockley, E. Richards, E. Peace, ? Williams, O.M.(?) Shelton and K. Williams. A few later became members of the St John Ambulance brigade. Of these, Muriel Bishop was not only devoted to the nursing profession (which she served for over twenty years) but also a talented artist. She often painted large scenery backdrops for pantomimes performed annually from the late 1940s by New Street Methodist Youth Club.

8th June, 1946

TO DAY, AS WE CELEBRATE VICTORY, I send this personal message to you and all other boys and girls at school. For you have shared in the hardships and dangers of a total war and you have shared no less in the triumph of the Allied Nations.

I know you will always feel proud to belong to a country which was capable of such supreme effort; proud, too, of parents and elder brothers and sisters who by their courage, endurance and enterprise brought victory. May these qualities be yours as you grow up and join in the common effort to establish among the nations of the world unity and peace.

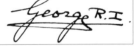

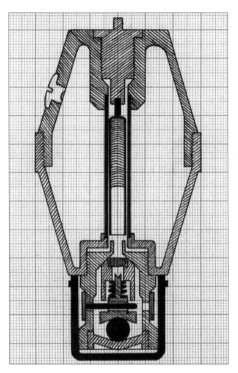

Left and below: A drawing of a hand grenade and notes taken by the author's father, Leslie Frost, while on an eventful munitions training course held at Dorking in 1943. Leslie was a draughtsman (with a keen eye for detail) at Sankey's and worked on the designs for Spitfire fuselages. He joined the Local Defence Volunteers (later to become the Home Guard) as a private and became munitions training officer for platoons in the district. He ended the war as a Second Lieutenant.

Opposite, above left: Charlie Parton of New Street was one of many volunteers to enlist in the Army. *Above right:* Upon his return from war, Charlie was presented with a book by the congregation of the Methodist church where his father was caretaker.

No.74. (Sticky Grenade). wt. (Gross 2½ lb.) without casing 2 lb.

A glass ball containing Nitro Glycerine in a plastic form (Consistency of Treacle), covered with stockinet, impregnated with a strong form of bird lime or roller latex, the whole protected by 2 metal hemispheres with a spring hinge, held in position by a clip or metal tape.

A hollow neck in the glass ball which takes the Igniter Set, consisting of a percussion cap, 5 second faze, detonator & primer. A bakelite handle containing the striker mechanism of the same design as the 36.

SAFETY PRECAUTIONS.

Before detonating see that Safety Pin is secure. See that Mushroom Head on top of Striker is securely fastened. See that percussion cap of Igniter Set does NOT project above housing this usually means that Detonator is tight in

container. It is liable to go of momentarily under the force of the striker. Reject if it cap projects.   Use Rubber bands to ensure that Igniter Set fits snugly in sleeve.

Rubber bands.   If the Nitro Glycerine comes into contact with skin it MUST be thoroughly removed or it will cause severe head aches. Should N.G. exude it must be wiped off and from inside sleeve.

The grenade must be lobbed with a follow-through action. A jerky movement is liable to break the glass neck.   Should the Grenade become stuck to a nearby object or person, before being thrown, the safety pin MUST be replaced & the Igniter Set removed before attempting to detach it.

BLINDS.

Handle comes off & Igniter Set falls out. Handle at too low an angle with safety lever underneath & so it can't fly off

To
C.E.B. PARTON

IN THANKFUL REMEMBRANCE OF YOUR SERVICE 1939 ~ 1945.

from

The Methodist Church, New Street, Wellington.

Wellington railway station saw a massive increase in traffic in the 1940s. Railways were vital to the war effort, not just for ferrying soldiers, sailors, airmen and government employees to their respective postings but also for transporting essential food, equipment, coal and other materials from one part of the country to another.

Above: Combined platoons of the local Home Guard parade through Market Square on Armistice Day, 1940. Armistice Day was commemorated even during the Second World War and was perhaps especially poignant in view of the numbers of local servicemen involved in hostilities at that time.

Left: An impromptu Victory in Europe (VE) parade in May 1945, walking past the Waverley Garage in King Street, with children from Prince's Street School and their parents. The garage and adjacent cottages (one of which was occupied by the Thomsett family) were subsequently demolished and replaced by Ron Bryan's Garage.

three

Celebrations

THE CHILDREN THANK YOU ONE AND ALL

The war ended in 1945 but Wellington would never be the same again. Almost everyone knew someone who had given their life or suffered injury to protect Britain or free another country. Those who had been engaged in war-related jobs, especially women, were reluctant to give up the relative independence attained by doing the sort of work that, before 1939, had been done solely by men. Post-war Britain did not deliver the promise of a 'land fit for heroes'. Many of those returning from the front found their jobs, despite promises, had been given to someone else or no longer existed.

However, this was not immediately apparent in 1945. This was a time for celebration. Impromptu victory parades sprang up from nowhere. A great feeling of relief swept through the country now that hostilities had ceased. Further minor, usually family-centred, celebrations took place in following years as more and more men returned from duty. Some establishments, like New Street Methodist church, gave souvenir books to members of the congregation who had served in the armed forces, as a token of appreciation for their patriotic efforts. The annual Wellington Carnival was revived, as were Christmas parties for the children of employees at factories such as Sankey's and Chad Valley. Despite continued austerity, there was a feeling of hope for a better future. By the early 1950s, restrictions were eased and commodities became more readily available. Wellington Smithfield reopened for livestock auctions in 1954 and brought considerably more trade to the town.

Another cause for celebration came with the Coronation of Queen Elizabeth II in 1953. Schoolchildren were given commemorative mugs or blue glass tumblers to mark the occasion. Wellington Urban District Council, as part of its town improvement strategy, arranged for All Saints parish churchyard, which appeared overgrown and unkempt after decades of neglect, to be given a facelift. (Thereafter, apart from rare interments in established family vaults, parish burials were confined to the public cemetery off Haygate Road. The parish churchyard became a Garden of Rest.) As with the cessation of hostilities in 1945, street parties were arranged for the benefit of children in the neighbourhood. Union Jack flags flew from poles erected in front gardens and from windows. It was as if Queen Elizabeth's accession to the throne somehow drew a line under the misery experienced during the 1940s. And, for the first time ever, people were able to witness the event from the comfort of their own homes by renting a television, then typically a large chunk of weighty furniture with a minuscule screen.

Television was regarded with some suspicion: although broadcasts were for a few hours daily, it was seen as the first stage in the destruction of family life, a conversation-stopper and a government propaganda machine. The Independent Television channel (ITV) in particular was regarded with disdain by many who refused to tune in, whatever the programme, and who felt it was promoted by companies wanting to sell you something you didn't want. ITV almost died an instant death in 1955 because of that attitude, but at least televisions had an off button.

Opposite above: Coronation celebrations at a street party held in Woollam Road, 2 June 1953.

Opposite below: Children, parents and organisers in a Coronation parade pass the former railway stationmaster's house in King Street. The parade ended with a party at the Union Free church, Constitution Hill. Roy Matthews, in his Boys' Brigade uniform, leads the way. One of the organisers, Colin Pitchford, holds the left pole of the banner.

Left: The original interior of New Street Methodist church was completely refurbished as part of the Coronation celebrations. The church, which was built in 1882, was demolished in 2003 and replaced by a modern multi-purpose building which opened in September 2004.

Below: The new Garden of Rest surrounding All Saints parish church is consecrated in a public service, 1953.

Trustee Savings Bank celebrated its new branch office in Walker Street in September 1951. It was opened by Wellington Urban District Council chairman Cecil Lowe (front, left). The first manager was E.S. Robinson (front, right).

Coronation night: a party for adults at Wrekin Services Club, 1953.

Birthdays are always a cause for celebration, as testified by this party for Carolyn Smith and Rosemary Sankey, probably held in the Charlton Arms Hotel, 1959. From left to right, back row: Ken Pearce, Dave Reid, -?-, -?-, Duncan Murphy, ? Brisborne, -?-. Middle row: -?-, John Peregrine, ? Brisborne, Nigel(?) Laird, Roger Ford, Jennifer Beaton, -?-, Veronica Whittles, Susan Norris, Elaine Daffern, -?-, -?-, -?-, Denzil Brisborne. Front row: Judy Jones, Susan Davidson, Carolyn Smith, Rosemary Sankey, Sue Kinna, Judy Fray, -?-.

four

Town
Developments

Armed with a seemingly bottomless pot of money made available by the government, Wellington Urban and Rural District Councils resumed their process of 'improving' the town and its environs. The intervention of war had led to the suspension of work which began in the 1930s. It was now time to continue and, in fact, expand the original plans.

Prior to 1939, development had been restricted to within the accepted boundaries of the town. There were still many slum properties, particularly in Glebe Street and High Street, but council planners became obsessed by a dream to create modern, concrete-based blocks of housing devoid of character at the expense of old cottages which could easily have been renovated to retain a traditional feel to the town.

These plans led to the issue of compulsory purchase orders, which were met with considerable hostility by affected businesses but, conversely, with some enthusiasm by the inhabitants of impoverished and dilapidated dwellings. Barber & Son were engaged by the council to submit valuations (as they were in the late 1960s when Telford Development Corporation embarked on its New Town project). A public hearing admonished the council for its inconsideration and high-handed approach but, while some businesses (like the author's family bakery in New Street) won their case and continued to trade, others (such as the Nelson Inn in High Street) were not so fortunate.

Ambitious projects were also undertaken on farmland to create vast areas of council (now euphemistically called 'social') housing on both sides of Dawley Road, the northern stretch of North Road and west of the gasworks. Private developments began in the southern part of North Road and Brooklands, with additional pockets elsewhere in the town.

These new estates were of enormous benefit to Wellington. They provided much better accommodation for council tenants, most of whom had probably never seen a bathroom or used electricity (which had, by now, replaced gas as the preferred means of heating and lighting but not, oddly enough, cooking) in their homes before.

Private housing was seen as essential to create a balance between the number of people represented by, or aspiring to, different social classes. Post-war wages were on the increase and so were some people's expectations for an improved standard of living. Owning your own house was a novel idea with a great deal of appeal yet, despite the gradual increase in car ownership, provision for a garage or a wider access road was seldom made. Planners seemed to have a gift for designing for the present but little concept of planning for future needs.

This period also witnessed the appearance of services intended to improve health in the community (for example, Meals on Wheels and a new babies' clinic in Haygate Road, which gave nutrition and health advice to mothers) as well as improved telegram deliveries for private and business customers alike.

Opposite below: Wellington Urban District Council and members of staff, 1958/59. Back row, fourth from left: Ron Briscoe. Fifth row, fourth from left: Billy Morris. Second row, fifth from left: Hubert Reece. Second row, extreme right: John Addison. From left to right, front row: -?-, Hugh Herdman, Philip Bott, -?-, Tom Edwards (chairman), Father Abbey, Ron Murphy, -?-, Ann Perry.

Above: Cottages in King Street bought by the council and left to become dilapidated before demolition, 1957. The house at the extreme right of the terrace was The Sun public house during the nineteenth century. On the right was James Tonks' coal merchants until J.E. England used the building as a potato warehouse. The Gregory family lived in the house (with television aerial) behind the entry. The road into School Court now occupies the site.

The Wellington Urban District Council office in Walker Street, opened in 1949. Since then it has served various purposes, including an Information Centre for visitors to the town.

The official opening of a new shopping precinct in Dawley Road by Cllr Alan Hartland, *c.* 1953. The precinct was intended to serve the needs of tenants in the massive new council house estates on adjacent land previously used for farming.

During the demolition of a cottage in High Street in 1955, Jim Childs (left) and his father Fred (right) discovered a woman's body hidden in a linen chest. It transpired that the woman's husband hid the body in order to continue to draw her pension.

Opening of Farcroft nursing home in North Road, 1959. Among the notables present was Tom Edwards (second from left), Wellington Urban District Council chairman at the time.

Left: Wellington Urban District Council chairman Cecil Lowe (back, centre) visits the first self-build house in Telford Road in the mid-1950s. The council actively encouraged small-scale developments which gave ordinary folk the chance to own their home. The 1950s also saw more widespread private development, especially in the Brooklands area of the town. Slowly but surely, the town's boundaries were being extended.

The council built several new public buildings as well as houses during the mid-1950s. *Above left:* Farcroft in North Road provided nursing for the elderly. *Left:* The police station relocated from restricted premises in Church Street to purpose-built offices in Glebe Street. These Divisional Police Headquarters were opened in October 1955 by Home Secretary Major the Right Honourable Gwilym Lloyd-George. *Below:* Wellington's fire brigade was provided with premises built on former farmland off Haybridge Road; it had previously been housed in Foundry Road.

Tax office staff at Belmont Hall, late 1950s. From left to right: Wilf Newton, Dick Knight, Mr Fuller, Jod Davies, Shirley Cooper-Edmunds, Bertie Rowlands.

Mothers and their babies meeting at the Welfare Food Office in Haygate Road, November 1951. From left to right, seated: Dr W.A.M. Stewart (Medical Officer of Health), T.E. Jury (District Food Executive Officer), Mrs Martin-Wilson OBE (Women's Voluntary Service county organiser), Cllr J.M. Hogan MBE, JP (Wellington Rural District Council chairman), Cecil Lowe (Wellington Urban District Council chairman). Standing, extreme left: A. Mountford (Regional Welfare Food Officer). Standing, extreme right: J.E. Woollam (Food Control Committee chairman).

Above and below: The first telegram in Shropshire to be delivered by motorcycle dispatch rider was sent by Cecil Lowe (centre), Wellington Urban District Council chairman, in February 1952. Head Postmaster H.M. Morrow (left) hands the envelope to John Shiels, who sits on a bright red Bantam motorcycle (complete with 'L' plates) outside the Walker Street post office. *Below:* The telegram was delivered to Wellington's oldest resident, Marion Jones, who was 103 years old when she died.

five

Business

Local businesses struggled to survive the 1940s. Those associated with entertainment did exceptionally well, a reflection of the fact that people needed an escape from reality at a time when wages were low and the future uncertain, and because there was little else to do. The Clifton, Grand and Town Hall cinemas allowed people to forget the real world for a time. The Clifton, opened in 1937, was also the venue for live performances in which, for example, choirs from all over the area united to entertain the public. Dancing to live music, as it had been for several years, was catered for by the former Palais de Danse (renamed the Majestic Ballroom in the late 1940s) in New Street and the Forest Glen Pavilion.

The majority of shops, especially those selling food and non-essential goods, were hit hard. Food rationing meant there was a limited amount available and prices were strictly controlled. Petrol rationing restricted travel and affected garages. Clothing shops were also hit by a lack of demand and, again, reduced supplies of material; people serving in the forces were supplied with uniforms and therefore didn't need to buy much in the way of civilian clothing ('civvies').

Folk were obliged to 'make do and mend' and not squander resources or their hard-earned cash. The government actively encouraged people to save, preferably by investing their money, however small the quantity, in war loans and bonds; it was not slow in appealing to patriotic feelings to promote this activity in support of the war effort. The fact that the money would never be returned was not a consideration. No government would be so devious as to go back on its promises.

The town's public houses, hotels and, of course, the Wrekin Brewery did particularly well, even though supplies of grain and hops could be unpredictable. Drink not only enhances the joy of celebration, it also provides solace in times of adversity. Women never entered a public house or even an hotel unescorted.

Market Square, looking north, 1940s.

Profits for most small traders were minimal until after the early years of the 1950s. The withdrawal of rationing in all its forms and increases in population and disposable earnings gave a long-awaited boost to the town's economy. Those involved with the building trade and home improvements did especially well: the council needed them for contract work and the householder wanted to improve the appearance of his castle, however modest.

Spare cash and an increase in leisure time encouraged the appearance of travel agents in the town. Whereas foreign travel was limited, there was plenty of scope for train or luxury coach travel and bed and breakfast accommodation in any of Britain's thriving, entertainment-packed seaside resorts.

Chats over tea or coffee, supplemented by a bun or fancy cake, became an established part of Wellington life. Conversations were a good way of catching up with local gossip or discussing national politics. Furthermore, shopping at a time when refrigerators were scarce and whatever food was available had to be brought fresh, often on a daily basis, was an arduous task and a few minutes' respite, perhaps while waiting for a bus or train home, was something of a high spot in the day. The Robin Hood Restaurant, located roughly where the public conveniences are now on the Parade car park, was opened by famous actress Phyllis Neilson-Terry in May 1943 as part of the government's aim to provide People's Restaurants, where nourishing food was supplied at cheap prices. It was no match for established cafés like Britain's in Market Square or the Mikado in Walker Street, yet managed to survive until the mid-1950s.

By the time 1959 arrived, the local economy, although still a trifle subdued, seemed set for marked improvement. Some shops had been unable to survive the last two decades; those that remained or had just opened, looked to the future with a greater degree of hope. War is so disruptive, so futile, yet Man never seems to learn. The Suez Crisis of 1956 was a sober reminder of how easy it can be for a nation to find itself involved in a conflict and for the lives of its people and profitability of businesses to be adversely affected.

Market Square, looking south, 1940s. Note the absence of road markings and the fact that traffic was allowed to move in both directions, even into New Street, where a car can be seen turning the corner.

Two familiar faces whose businesses took them all over the town. *Left:* Milkman Fred Treherne of Victoria Avenue, who delivered milk in buckets and jugs until glass bottles became the norm in the 1950s. *Above:* Chimney sweep Chlours Twinney of Glebe Street. Almost every house had a coal fire.

Eddie Woodcock helped Bob Stirling, an employee of Noah Frost & Sons of New Street, to deliver bread around the town in the early 1950s. The house he is delivering to, Orleton Cottage, was the home of Wellington historian George Evans' parents at the time.

Above: The popular Mikado café, which served delicious cakes, and Potts' shoe shop in Walker Street, 1949.

Left: Elaine Speed stands in the entrance to her father Sidney's grocery shop in Wrekin Road, *c.* 1940. The shop sold individual sweets for a farthing and was a particular favourite with children attending Wrekin Road Junior School over the road. Mr Speed moved into former W.J. Laud's bakery premises a few doors away in the early 1960s.

Fresh fish supplied daily, mainly transported by train from Grimsby, on sale at Mac Fisheries in New Street, 1950s. It was impossible to pass by without noticing the smell! Rabbits (hanging on display), pigeons and poultry were also sold.

Brown's in New Street, next door to the Palais de Danse (renamed the Majestic Ballroom in the late 1940s), provided hire cars as well as taxi and funeral services. This advertising photograph was taken in 1944.

Wellington Laundry was patronised by many businesses and individuals requiring the highest standards and prompt service. The laundry ran several regular routes around the town and neighbourhood. Like similar businesses at the time, the firm was obliged to embrace dry-cleaning processes and opened a shop in Market Square to keep abreast of changing customer demands.

Above left: Agnew's tailors in former post office premises in Church Street, 1947.

Above right: Percy Jones' grocery shop in Watling Street, with an awning typical in the town at this time. After his death, his brother George sold leather goods, toys and bread here. The adjacent building was used by Reade's Garage and was formerly the Prince of Wales public house until some time before the First World War. Next to it is the timber-framed Swan Inn (rebuilt in 1960) and, on the extreme left, the Cock Hotel, a meeting place for campaigners against the slave trade in the late 1700s.

Alf Davies stands outside his grocery shop in the new shopping development on Dawley Road, mid-1950s. Food preservation during the war had led to the increased use of cans such as those displayed in the window.

A letterhead from Norah Wellings' toy works, 1940s. The world-renowned factory closed in 1959 and was sold in June 1960 to make way for new housing and an Esso petrol station in King Street.

Interior of Woolworths, 1940s. The company had arrived in Wellington during the 1930s and built a new store on a site previously occupied by small shops, including Arthur's bakery. Note the unlit gas lamps hanging between newly installed electric lights: they proved useful during electric power outages even as late as the 1980s.

Right: Post office buildings in Walker Street, 1944. The gate to the right was used by delivery vans, bicycles and motorcycles and provided access to the main sorting office at that time.

Below: Percy Davies, a familiar face at Wellington Market Hall, mid-1950s. The hall was built in 1868 to provide a large under-cover amenity for traders and shoppers alike. At that time, market days were restricted to Thursdays and Saturdays.

Wellington Journal & Shrewsbury News staff with their delivery van and trailer, 1958. From left to right: Messrs Treherne, Osbourne, Parton and Parton.

The corner of Church Street and Queen Street, *c.* 1950. Agnew's outfitters is on the left, next door to R. Partridge's newsagents, with the *Wellington Journal & Shrewsbury News* office on the corner. The angled doorway also gave access to dentists on the upper floor and is now the entrance to Churchill's Bar. W. Brindley's Popular Café tea rooms in Queen Street, which gave sustenance to passengers awaiting Midland Red bus services, can just be seen in the distance.

Wright's grocery shop on the corner of King Street and Victoria Street was popular with children at Constitution Hill School; they grasped the opportunity to buy sweets with the threepenny bits gained when glass fizzy pop bottles were returned. The bus is one operated by T.G. Smith between Wellington and Donnington and is a 1947 Daimler CVD6 which worked the route until 1963.

The Forest Glen Pavilion, seen here in the 1940s, was a very popular venue for day-trippers, especially on bank holidays when regular bus services ran from Wellington. It provided refreshment to those who had just climbed The Wrekin Hill, as well as being the preferred venue for countless dinner parties, dances and wedding receptions. The battered body of a young ATS woman, assumed to have been murdered by an American soldier, was discovered here during a wartime dance in 1942. The chief suspect was found not guilty but was sent back to America with unseemly haste.

Above: The Shropshire Works of R. Groom & Sons, a thriving timber business alongside the railway sidings. The enterprise was founded by Richard Groom, a staunch Methodist, in the first half of the nineteenth century.

New shops on Dawley Road, seen here in the mid-1950s, were created as an essential amenity to the residents of the extensive housing estates at Kingsland, Arleston and off Dawley Road itself. These premises were ideal for small businesses at a time when supermarkets and out-of-town shopping centres hadn't even been considered.

Above: The Lido Hotel, Haygate Road, had an open-air swimming pool in which the owner of Wrekin Rose Nursery (whose greenhouses can be seen to the right of the photograph) committed suicide. The building had a short life as a hotel and was bought by Dr Rose, an orthopaedic surgeon at the Royal Salop Infirmary at Shrewsbury, in 1950. Several garden parties for New Street Methodist church were held here in the mid-1950s.

Opposite below: This receipt from R. Groom & Sons shows the range of wooden products available in 1947. At one time, the firm was the largest supplier of timber (both indigenous and imported) in Britain. The factory was closed in 1970.

Left: John Childs (in the foreground) died while working as a farmhand at Hollybush Farm in 1946. The farm buildings, complete with stables and cellars, had been used until the mid-nineteenth century as an inn and coach house for travelling tradesmen and wagoners. The farm's land was acquired to create the Boys' Grammar School and housing along Golf Links Lane during the 1940s, although the stables continued to provide horse-riding facilities.

Below: Members of Longdon upon Tern church choir enjoy a meal at the Robin Hood People's Restaurant, *c.* 1950. The restaurant opened in May 1943 and over 250 meals were served on the first day. It closed in the early 1950s and was located where the public conveniences are now on the Parade car park.

six

Transport

Before 1950, there were few people with their own transport apart from a bicycle or, for those in business, a van of one size or another. Horse-drawn vans and carriages had largely been replaced by motorised vehicles during the 1930s, although a few, most notably coal merchants, would be seen trotting laboriously around the town for a few more years. The remarkable thing about delivery horses was that they knew their route as well as the driver and invariably stopped at the next customer's house without the reins having to be pulled.

Apart from the humble bicycle, serviced either at home with a puncture repair kit and can of Three-in-One oil stored in a small pouch hanging from the back of the seat, or by Bill Perry in Park Street or Gordon Lees in Victoria Street, the next step up the mobility ladder was a motorcycle, perhaps with a sidecar. These required considerably more mechanical know-how, well beyond the capability of most riders of the time, so the services of Doran and Wright in Whitchurch Road or Harry Stanford in King Street were the first ports of call in an emergency. Very few people owned motor cars until the 1950s, a period which witnessed a slow but sure end to years of extreme austerity.

Wartime leisure travel was discouraged. Non-essential journeys were a waste of limited resources. Petrol rationing had to be strictly controlled to ensure emergency services and military activities were not compromised. It made life very difficult.

Long-distance travel was predominantly by rail, both for passengers and goods. Wellington station, with its close proximity to the newly constructed Civilian Ordnance Depot at Donnington (see *Donnington and Muxton* by the same author) and countless camps, airfields and other government establishments, saw a massive increase in the number of people travelling into and out of the area. Even animals were brought to Wellington Smithfield, which had its own loading bays on the side of the tracks, by train, before being reloaded into wagons for distribution to slaughterhouses and farms throughout the country.

Travellers changed trains at Wellington to continue their journeys on branch lines serving, for example, High Ercall, Donnington and Much Wenlock. Many smaller villages were provided with a platform in the middle of nowhere and very few other facilities. Stopping a train at these halts often meant sticking an arm out as a train approached.

The main mode of transport for most people was the bus. Unfortunately, there was more than a hint of rivalry between the Midland Red Omnibus Co., whose fleet operated mainly from Queen and Charlton Streets, and small, privately owned operators (who had jointly formed the Shropshire Omnibus Association during the 1930s to protect their interests), whose services terminated in Victoria Street. John Jervis operated from Wellington (his garage was off Regent Street) while most other members were based elsewhere in the neighbourhood. Squabbles between competing operators had been, and would continue to be, a frequent occurrence. Some drivers deliberately loitered beyond their scheduled departure time or crawled along their set routes, hoping to snatch passengers intending to catch the following bus.

There were two major problems at both the Queen Street and Victoria Street termini. One was that there were no clocks for passengers or drivers to check the time. The second was that no provision had been made for people to wait under cover; when it rained, they had no choice but to get wet. After several years of wrangling (even over who would be responsible for maintaining the clocks), these facilities were installed by the early 1950s, when passenger numbers were set to rise after a post-war decline. The decline was not so great or long-lasting as expected. Post-war services were still needed to serve COD Donnington, as well as other large employers like Sankey's at Hadley. Wellington had traditionally been the place to which inhabitants of the surrounding area came for shopping and entertainment. Increasing relative prosperity during the 1950s saw a corresponding increase in passengers visiting the town. Cessation of hostilities and the eventual suspension of petrol rationing also enabled travel further afield without restriction.

Another notable feature of travel was that coach tours and coach holidays became a popular means of getting away. Whereas buses provided a basic and often uncomfortable means of travelling short distances, coaches with padded seats made long-distance journeys and evening mystery drives something of an exciting experience, even if there were no restrictions on smoking inside. Transport cafés, such as the Shamrock at Overley Hill, sprang up like mushrooms outside towns and along major roads. Their amenities may not have been too hygienic but hardened travellers were used to making do when the need arose.

The war provided the opportunity for many folk, including women, to learn how to drive. The 1950s saw a gradual rise in the numbers purchasing their own cars and, where the cost was too prohibitive, actually hiring them for the day to take their families into the countryside. From now on, such freedoms would be taken for granted. No longer would the general population be confined to live out their lives in the township in which they had been born.

In much the same way as bicycles and motorcycles had made specialist services economically worthwhile, the 1950s saw an increase in the prosperity and feasibility of garages of one sort or another. Petrol and servicing might be provided in one garage, another might sell and service new and second-hand cars but not sell petrol. A few mechanics did repairs as a sideline. It wasn't until the 1960s that petrol stations, which did nothing other than sell petrol (and sweets) and provide free compressed air for deflated tyres, became commonplace.

The author stands on the eastbound platform of Wellington station, *c.* 1956. His brother, David, was a keen trainspotter. It wasn't a universally popular pastime.

Railway carriage cleaners' cabin (a former clerestory coach) at Wellington, *c.* 1957. The barrels and drum contain various cleaning fluids and machine oil. From left to right: Don Houlston (fireman) and Joe Watkins (former driver at Much Wenlock until the shed there closed in 1951).

Members of railway staff outside one of Wellington station's sheds in the 1950s.

One of John Jervis's buses at a passenger stand in Victoria Avenue. This one ran a service to Priorslee via Oakengates. Bus operators paid a fee to run the same routes; if an operator's service became too unreliable or he went out of business, other members of the Shropshire Omnibus Association would bid to take it over.

Mechanics and staff at Blackhams, seen here at their premises off Spring Hill, 1950s. Blackhams began business in a workshop off Victoria Street and took the decision to move to these larger premises as a result of increased car ownership.

Reade's Watling Street Garage, *c*. 1952. The garage began in the early 1920s and had been constructed in the small area known as The Rookery. Whereas the Swan Inn (on the left) had been built originally to serve the needs of medieval travellers, Reade's Garage provided fuel and repair services for motorists in the twentieth century. The buildings were subsequently replaced and the business became a Renault car dealership. It is currently the site of Wiley & Holland, motorcycle dealers. The corner doorway on the right was the main door into the Prince of Wales public house.

The Cock Hotel junction on the A5 did not cater well for large vehicles, especially this one transporting a load from Adamson Butterley of Horsehay in the 1950s. Reade's Garage had to remove petrol pumps temporarily to allow it to turn from Dawley Road into Watling Street.

The Cock Hotel (left) and Swan Inn (right) crossroads, mid-1950s. This was a major junction for traffic travelling along north-south and east-west routes and the traffic island increasingly caused bottlenecks, especially during bank holiday and summer holiday periods. Traffic lights replaced the island in 1958. The building behind the island was, until 1916, the Anchor public house; the site is now part of the Swan Hotel car park.

The Buck's Head crossroads, looking east, 1950s. Signposts removed during the war years to confuse the enemy were replaced and a depot for British Road Services opened; in time, road haulage would replace rail as the preferred means of transporting goods from one part of the country to another. As with the Cock Hotel crossroads, traffic lights eventually helped ease traffic congestion.

TELEPHONE 31

GLEBE STREET GARAGE
and CAR HIRE (Council Car Park South Entrance)

WELLINGTON'S REAL SERVICE STATION

OPEN ALL NIGHT — PETROL - REPAIRS - SPARES

BENNETTS BANK GARAGE
G. M. Taylor, *Motor Engineer*

RE-BORING AND TUNING A SPECIALITY	**WELLINGTON SHROPSHIRE**	CARS WASHED AND GREASED

CARS OVERHAULED AND REPAIRED

P. PIERCE ERCALL GARAGE LTD.

MAIN AGENTS for	APPOINTED R.A.C. AGENTS
MORRIS	A.A. REPAIRERS
WOLSELEY	—
HILLMAN	COMPLETE OVERHAULS
HUMBER	by
SUNBEAM TALBOT	Fully Skilled Mechanics
COMMER	

EFFICIENT   SERVICE

LUCAS BATTERY SERVICE STATION	COACH PAINTING
—	CELLULOSING
GIRLING DEPOT	and
—	ALL BODY REPAIRS
CARS FOR HIRE	UNDERTAKEN

MARKET STREET
WELLINGTON

Phone 96   Phone 96

M.A.A.   *B.M.T.A.*

JAMES BROTHERS
(Wellington) LTD.

Complete Overhauls Tractors and Lorries
※
Acetylene and Electric Welding
※
Tools and Equipment Lubricating Oil Tyres
※
Sales and Service

AGRICULTURAL and MOTOR ENGINEERS

Foundry Road
Wellington
Shropshire

Telephone : WELLINGTON 877

Above and below: Advertisements for local garages and cycle shops, 1950. Some were able to supply vehicles, others maintain them. A few were able to provide both services.

QUEEN'S GARAGE
WELLINGTON   -   SHROPSHIRE
Prop. : A. T. BETHELL

Auto-Electrical   Engineer

FOR SERVICE and SATISFACTION
Telephone : 875 WELLINGTON

VEHICLE SUPPLIERS & REPAIRERS, 1954

Garages and repairs
BENNETT'S BANK GARAGE
BROWN, E. & SON
   New Street Garage (Tel. 343)
CHETWOOD'S LTD.
   Tan Bank Garage
GLEBE STREET GARAGE (Hal Jones)
   White House
JAMES BROS (Wellington) LTD
   Foundry Road & King Street
PARK STREET GARAGE (Doran, Bill & Wright, Matt)
PIERCE, P, ERCALL GARAGE
   Market Street
QUEEN'S GARAGE (A T Bethel)
   Walker Street
READE'S GARAGE (WELLINGTON) LTD
   Watling Street (Tel. 162)
VICTORIA MOTOR CO.
   Victoria Street
WAVERLEY GARAGE (WELLINGTON) LTD.
   Church Street

Bicycles and Motorcycles
DORAN, MATT & WRIGHT, BILL
   Park Street Garage. (Tel. 138)
GORDON LEES
   Victoria Street
PERRY, BILL
   Park Street
PURSLOW (of Shrewsbury)
   King Street & Victoria Street

You see more Austins on the roads of Britain today than any other single make of car

The A40—a champion dollar earner for Britain

Among the many very early Austin models—old in everything but performance—that you see on the go today are the 'Baby' Austins, the indomitable little Sevens. A Sussex owner of a 1926 model says :

" It is still in perfect running order and was only recently re-bored for the first time, despite the fact that it is used every day over many rough roads. In my opinion the car is a wonderful advertisement for the workmanship of Austins."

And much the same will be said in the future about the new Austin A40 'Devon' saloon, for it, too, is built to give you years and years of willing service.

The 1926 Austin 'Seven'

AN **AUSTIN** LASTS LONGER
—you can depend on it!

THE WAVERLEY GARAGE (Wellington) Ltd.
Church Street, Wellington
Phone 53 and 747

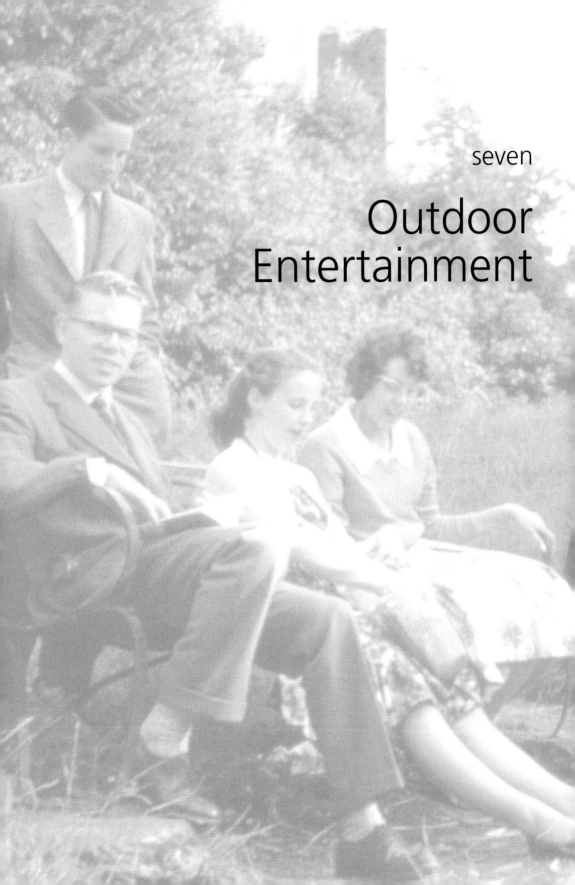

seven

Outdoor
Entertainment

During the war years people were satisfied with what would be regarded as very simple entertainment today; they had little choice. Even a trip to Shrewsbury on a train or bus could cause excitement. Very few people had televisions and thus most entertainment had to be created by and for themselves. Walks and picnics up the Ercall and Wrekin Hills were a regular feature and, once petrol rationing ended, mystery coach trips in the evenings to such exotic places as Ludlow, Much Wenlock and Carding Mill Valley, near Church Stretton, were laid on by church congregations and other groups. Excursions to seaside resorts, Eyton horse races, football matches and other attractions increased their frequency during the 1950s. Trips were also enjoyed by Sunday School children as part of their annual treat for regular attendance. Even British Railways laid on special excursion trains on bank holidays, throughout the summer and at Christmas.

The Wrekin Hill was, to many locals, the most popular outdoor local attraction. On bank holidays, regular bus services ferried casual walkers of all ages to the Forest Glen Pavilion. Others might cycle there or walk along Ercall Lane before embarking on the not-too-arduous trek to the summit, where touching the trigonometric concrete pillar became a symbol of success. Other, less portly, people might also venture to squeeze through the Needle's Eye, a natural crevice in a rocky outcrop near the summit. The views were, and still are, staggering in all directions, provided the weather is good. Visits were not limited to summer months, when picnics were the order of the day; snow brought home-made sledges out of the back of the coal shed for their annual airing. Furthermore, walks were not confined to daylight hours: members of New Street Methodist Youth Club, for example, made seeing the sun rise from the summit on Midsummer's Day an annual event. Whatever the weather, The Wrekin Hill holds an attraction to so many people and has been a public playground for centuries. On the way up (or, more deservedly, on the way down), walkers were tempted to take refreshment at the Halfway House while younger visitors rode on a donkey or in swingle boats. Essential amenities (toilets) were available both here and at the Forest Glen.

Less ambitious ramblers took walks through the Ercall Hill or along Lime Kiln Lane and thence into the Short Woods (taking care to avoid sloping adits into shallow coal mines) or onto the golf course, or to The Hatch. Lime Kiln Lane had been a popular route for courting couples during the 1920s and 1930s; by the 1940s, it had become a favourite with children. In those days (and, indeed, until the 1960s), parents had no qualms about their offspring spending whole days playing in the woods south of the town. Fossil-hunting in disused lime pits was another activity enjoyed by more adventurous (or more foolhardy) folk, including the author.

The annual town carnival, whose proceeds went to a charity chosen by the chairman of the council, were revived as soon as the war ended. They took place around the Whitsun holiday weekend, and always on a Saturday. These carnivals were strongly supported by local businesses and inhabitants alike. Lorries were transformed into imaginative, highly decorated floats, led through the streets by army and local bands, dance troops and individuals dressed as indians, cowboys, clowns and so on, each wielding a bucket in which to collect every penny of loose change from crowds of onlookers. The parade invariably terminated at the Buck's Head football ground, where further entertainment in the form of sports, displays and fireworks brought the day's exciting proceedings to a close.

Another annual event revived after the war was the Wrekin Fête, also known as the Wrekin Fête and Wellington Horse and Pony Show (many landowners, farmers and successful businessmen had horses, if only to keep their daughters happy). The fête, which continued into the 1950s, took place in the grounds of Col. Herbert's Orleton Hall on the western outskirts of Wellington. There were many attractions besides the obligatory horse and pony competitions: sack racing for children aged under eighteen, potato racing and musical chairs for all ages, boxing (Randolph Turpin took part in 1952), motorcycle demonstrations (by Demon Bill Deegan and Hell's Angels), mannequin parades and children's dancing displays. Sankey's Hadley Castle Works Broadcasting Band provided music while folk played skittles (to win a pig) and Aunt Sally, shot crows (not real ones!), threw at coconut shies or fished for 'ducks' while performances of marionettes (by Clement Minns of London) or a conjuror (such as Professor Gazeka with his magic carpet) took place. Other entertainment was provided by well-known radio comedians such as Frank Harris, musicians such as George Clay, virtuoso of the accordion, and singers such as Florence Wilson and Arthur Bayliss. The Baby Show was extremely well supported. Beer was invariably dispensed in crowded, smoke-filled marquees by the Wrekin Brewery.

Other special events took place from time to time, although not necessarily on an annual or even regular basis. Starved of much opportunity for enjoyment during the war years, Wellingtonians afterwards seized every opportunity to take part in or attend every event organised for them. In 1956, for example, a Horse Show was held at the Buck's Head football ground, supplemented by a range of sideshows and displays in much the same way, although on a much smaller scale, as the Wrekin Fête. Presumably the pitch was scrupulously cleaned before the next football match was due to be played.

On an even smaller scale, churchgoers of, for example, New Street Methodist church, organised garden parties, normally held in the grounds of one of their member's homes. These events were held to raise money for church funds and included several sideshows (such as pseudo-fortune tellers and John Giles' Marionette Theatre), games like skittles and hoopla as well as tombola and cake stalls. If nothing else, they provided a good opportunity for adults to relax and chat in pleasant surroundings while children took part in activities.

Then, of course, came the travelling fairground in early December and the occasional circus. Both were highly popular.

Peter Wheatley (lying prone on a makeshift stretcher fitted to a bicycle, cunningly devised by Scouts) takes part in a first-aid display at an event held at the Buck's Head football ground, 1954. Harley Jones is standing next to him.

Jim Bishop was responsible for the maintenance of the beacon on top of The Wrekin Hill after it was erected in the early 1940s. He is pictured here with one of the donkeys used to provide rides for children at the Halfway House (or Wrekin Cottage as it was properly named). Behind him are the highly popular swingle boats. The Halfway House provided refreshments as well as entertainment for hill walkers.

Coach outings were quite common for the employees of larger businesses throughout the period. Here, Gas Board staff take a break on their annual trip in the early 1950s.

Opposite below: An evening trip for members of New Street Methodist church, *c.* 1959. Seated on the left, nearest the camera, are Ida and Ken Jones, leaders of the church's youth club. Behind them are Gert and Bill Davis. The couple on the right are Neville Archer and Vivien Taylor. Marjorie and Ken Roberts can just be seen on either side of the aisle at the back. Ken and Vivien are reading the *Express and Star*, the Wolverhampton-produced evening newspaper which preceded the *Shropshire Star*.

Above: A New Street Methodist Youth Club coach outing to Ludlow Castle, 1959. Standing: Ken Poulter. Seated, from left to right: -?-, Pat Danks, Wendy Hancox, Colin Lane.

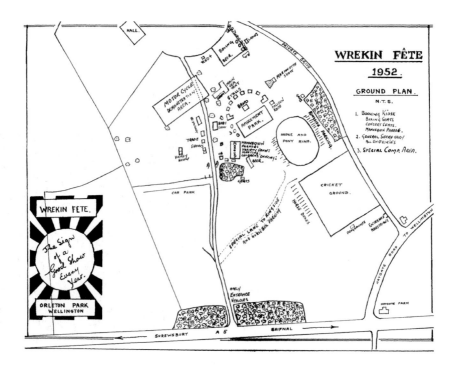

A plan of the grounds of Orleton Park, on the western outskirts of Wellington, showing the layout of the various entertainments for the 1952 fête. Fêtes and shows had been immensely popular here since the 1930s and continued into the 1950s.

Wrekin Fête, 1952. Proud mothers with their offspring await the judging of the Baby Competition.

Opposite page: A programme cover for the 1956 Wellington Horse Show, organised by well-known personalities in the town.

Wellington (Shropshire) Horse Show

(Under B.S.J.A. Rules)

Football Ground, Wellington
Saturday, 30th June, 1956

President :
J. T. STONE, Esq.

Judges (B.S.J.A.)
R. BELCHER, Esq.   R. F. TANNER, Esq.
H. J. DAVIES, Esq.   E. TURNER, Esq.

Ring Marshalls :
N. WYCHERLEY, Esq.   J. H. GRIFFITHS, Esq.

Collecting Ring Steward :
W. MINTON, Esq.

Medical Officers :
Doctors :-- H. W. BAMBRIDGE.   D. HEWAT-JABOOR
J. S. REDFERN

Veterinary Surgeons :
K. SCOTT, Esq.   T. JARVIS, Esq.   H. SIMPSON, Esq.
M.R.C.V.S   M.R.C.V.S.   M.R.C.V.S.

Hon. Farrier :
J. NAGINGTON, Esq.

Committee :
J. P. FORD (Chairman),   J. C. FOULKES (Vice-Chairman)
N. WYCHERLEY,   R. E. BEBB,   J. H. GRIFFITHS,
E. DORRELL,   R. V. DRURY,   P. BRISBOURNE,
S. J. L. ROBERTS.

Hon. Treasurer :
F. NAGINGTON, Esq.

Hon, Secretary :
O. L. SAXTON, Esq.

Asst. Show Secretaries :
Miss M. COLEMAN and R. E. EAST, Esq.

British Show Jumping Association Local Representative :
H. C. CORNES, Esq.

Souvenir Programme   =   Sixpence

Above: Wellington Carnival, *c.* 1957. Noddy in Toyland wins second prize in the non-commercial float category.

The Boys' Brigade, based at Tan Bank Methodist chapel, march up High Street towards Mill Bank, *c.* 1950. The brigade paraded around the town once a month, finishing their march at the chapel just in time for the Sunday morning service.

Children living in the same neighbourhood tended to play together, often venturing into areas not entirely safe. This intrepid group, all of whom lived in King Street near the Drill Hall, are at the top of the railway embankment by Waterloo Road. From left to right, back row: Michael Parton, Graham Parton, Nigel Pitchford. Front row: Stephen Parton, Sandy the dog, the author. The author's brother, David, took the photograph in 1955. Nigel is wearing a snake belt, an elasticated belt with an S-shaped buckle, very popular at the time.

Opposite below: Crowds line King Street as bands lead the carnival parade southwards past All Saints parish churchyard, 1956.

Left: The gatehouse to Orleton Hall. The hall grounds were the venue for annual Wrekin Fêtes until the 1950s. Well organised and with a wide variety of attractions (including beer tents), these fêtes were highly popular and brought visitors and important guests from far afield. Grounds adjoining Haygate Road became the pitch for Wellington Cricket Club in the late 1940s.

Below: One of the most popular outdoor activities suitable for all the family was a leisurely walk up The Wrekin Hill, seen here in the 1950s. The views from the top were (and still are) superb. Wellington can be seen in the distance while the Ercall Hill dominates the centre background.

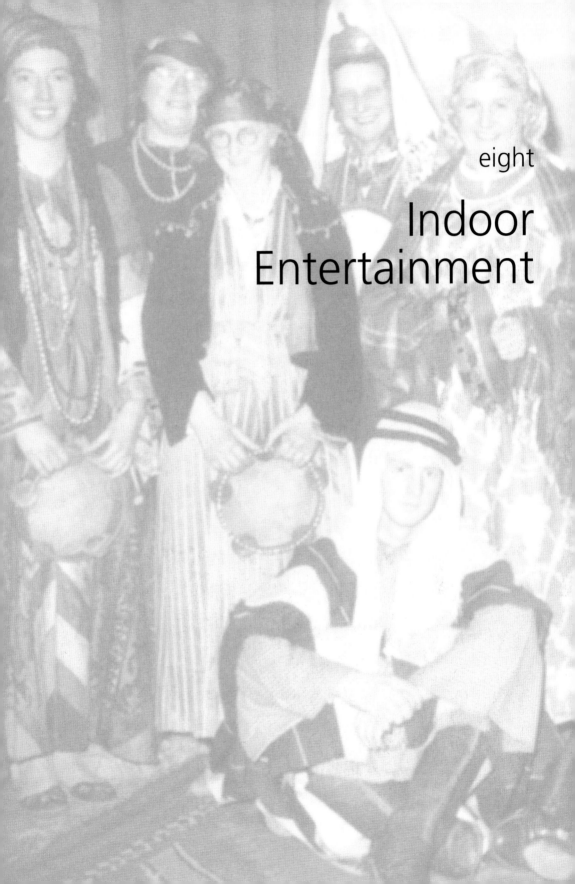

eight

Indoor
Entertainment

Entertainment was a vital morale-booster during the dark years of the war. As there was little else to do outdoors in evenings because of the blackout, people flocked in their hundreds to the cinemas and dance halls. Travel from outlying districts was by both train and bus, neither of which had been prepared to cater for the numbers involved. The rush for last buses at the Queen Street and Victoria Street termini had to be seen to be believed! Despite constant wrangling for additional rations of petrol, bus companies managed to satisfy customers by putting on, whenever possible, additional vehicles. As had been the case since the early 1930s, local bus operators were in constant battle with the Birmingham-based Midland Red Omnibus Co., especially over allegations of 'poaching' customers.

It wasn't until well after the war that shelters were erected at both termini. Before then, passengers had to wait in the open air, whatever the weather. For girls, failure to catch the last bus (at around ten o'clock) could mean incurring a father's wrath. Brown's taxi service near the Palais de Danse in New Street couldn't hope to cope with demand, so catching the bus or train was vital. Dances were also held at the Drill Hall in King Street on a fairly regular basis and at the Forest Glen Pavilion.

Many paid regular visits to the 'flicks' at the Grand Theatre or the Clifton or Town Hall cinemas. Double seats were very popular with courting couples, especially at the Grand, whatever film was showing. On the other hand, the Town Hall began to resemble a fleapit, where the risk of fire was ever-present. People also attended societies and other groups in search of entertainment; the 1940s saw an upsurge in the number of indoor events for the general public to enjoy.

Several churches provided various forms of entertainment, not just for their own members but also for forces personnel and government civilian employees. It was hard for the latter to be moved away from their homes and families to an area with which they were totally unfamiliar but the local population, by and large, did its best to make them feel welcome.

Such was the success of some of these enterprises that, after 1945, permanent youth clubs were established, not only at New Street Methodist church but also a council-run one at Constitution Hill School. The Young Men's Christian Association (YMCA) had been operating in the town for many decades, most recently from their building at the junction of Tan Bank and Walker Street. Clubs provided an alternative to public house activities and gained excellent reputations for their organisational abilities as well as their facilities. Football teams, including those of the YMCA, played in local leagues. Matball, cricket and rounders teams were also popular, as were athletics competitions.

One of the most successful organisations to give guidance and enjoyment to youngsters was the Scouting movement, which had groups at All Saints parish church as well as at the new Boys' Grammar School in Golf Links Lane. Tan Bank Methodist chapel had its own Boys' Brigade, whose band marched through the town once a month on its way to morning service. Girls were catered for by the Girl Guide Association. Members of these organisations were occasionally called upon to appear at carnivals and shows, where they played music, marched or gave displays of useful subjects like first aid.

In addition to clubs, other societies, many of which had been in existence well before 1939, continued to flourish. The Caged Bird Society met at, and several dog shows took place in, the Drill Hall in King Street, while railway workers belonging to the Wellington Loco Horticultural Society held an annual show inside the Station Hotel.

Children were well catered for. As well as youth clubs, Scouts and Guides, several specialised groups sought to provide alternative enjoyment for the offspring of parents wishing to enrich their children's lives. Dance classes were very well attended and gave participants an added thrill by putting on performances to show the ability of their pupils.

By April 1947, elderly residents of the town began to feel left out and launched a campaign for the formation of their own club. The result was the Darby and Joan Club, which attracted an immediate membership of over fifty people, meeting once a week for two hours at All Saints parish church hall. After two years, they managed to raise the money to buy their own black and white hut (assisted by members of the Wellington branch of the Toc H society) in Wrekin Road. As the years went by, it became apparent that larger premises were needed, especially since the council had grand plans to redevelop parts of the town, but they had to wait until 1961 to take up residence in a newly constructed building at Belmont Hall. This was built on the site of a former timber sports pavilion in the grounds of the original Belmont, once home to Rowland Barber (son of John Barber, who founded Barber's, currently the oldest established firm in Wellington), which was demolished in 1967.

An extract from Foundry Road-based Wellington fire brigade's Incident Book, 1942. The Town Hall cinema could easily have witnessed more dangerous incidents: many former patrons remember having to peer through dense cigarette, cigar and pipe smoke in an effort to watch the big screen. Dog-ends and ash were dropped onto the floor along with ice-cream wrappers and tubs.

The Clifton cinema in the 1950s. It is currently a Dunelm soft-furnishings store.

The Clifton cinema didn't just show films: it also hosted live variety performances, as well as this March 1941 production of Handel's *Messiah*, performed by local church choirs, the Hadley Orpheus and Donnington Orpheus Societies to an audience of 1,200. From left to right, front row: Parry Jones (tenor), Freda Townson (contralto), Major Arnold Fulton (conductor), Olive Groves (soprano).

Opposite below: Both sides of a foldover ticket for a dance at the Majestic Ballroom, 1950. Live dance music at that time lasted considerably longer than today's equivalents. The 'Partners' column ensured participants were not double-booked for a dance.

```
┌─────────────────────────────────────────────────────────────────────────────┐
│                        :: PROGRAMME ::                                        │
├──────────────────┬──────────────────────────────────┬───────────────────────┤
```

THURSDAY, APRIL 2nd. Three Days.	Matinee Saturday **THE GREAT DICTATOR** ⓤ	CHARLES CHAPLIN with Paulette Goddard
MONDAY, APRIL 6th. Three Days. Last C.P.—7-15.	Matinee Monday **GIRLS AT SEA** ⓤ (Technicolor) **GUNSMOKE IN TUCSON** (U) (CinemaScope—Color)	RONALD SHINER GUY ROLFE Mark Stevens Forrest Tucker
THURSDAY, APRIL 9th. Three Days.	Matinee Saturday **PLEASE SEE LOCAL PRESS.**	
MONDAY, APRIL 13th. Three Days. Last C.P.—6-50.	Matinee Monday **THE SIGN OF ZORRO** ⓤ **THE LIGHT IN THE FOREST** (U) (Technicolor)	GUY WILLIAMS HENRY CALVIN Fess Parker Wendell Corey Joanne Dru
THURSDAY, APRIL 16th. Three Days. Last C.P.—6-50.	Matinee Saturday **I WAS MONTY'S DOUBLE** ⓤ 1-55, 5-10, 8-30. **COLE YOUNGER, GUNFIGHTER** (U) (CinemaScope—Color)	JOHN MILLS CECIL PARKER CLIFTON JAMES Frank Lovejoy Abby Dalton
MONDAY, APRIL 20th. Six Days. Last C.P.—7-10.	Matinees Monday, Saturday **THE INN OF THE SIXTH HAPPINESS** ⓤ (CinemaScope — EastmanColor) Screened at 1-15. 4-25, 7-35.	INGRID BERGMAN CURT JURGENS ROBERT DONAT
MONDAY, APRIL 27th. Six Days	Matinees Monday, Saturday **CARRY ON NURSE** ⓤ	SHIRLEY EATON KENNETH CONNOR

Above: Advertising leaflets let the viewing public know what films were due to be screened the following month. This one was produced by the Clifton cinema in 1959. A few of the main feature films have stood the test of time, unlike the 'B' movies.

THE MAJESTIC
WELLINGTON

Future Dates

March 3
March 24
April 14
April 21
May 5
May 19 Special Visit of Harry Davidson and his Band —Opening of Hall Extension
June 2
June 16
June 30

DANCING

Every

THURSDAY

7-30 p.m. to 11 p.m.

ADMISSION 2'-

and

SATURDAY

7-30 p.m. to 11 p.m.

ADMISSION 2'6

Olde Tyme
Ball 24

Friday,
17th February

Music by
CYRIL BIRMINGHAM
and his
Electronics Dance Orchestra

Modern Lounge & Buffet

DANCING
8 p.m. until midnight
M.C. : T. JACQUES

Admission - 3/-

See back of programme for future dates

PROGRAMME		PARTNERS
1. Waltz	.....	
2. Military Two Step	.....	
3. Royal Minuet	.....	
4. Latchford Schottische	.....	
5. Blue Danube Waltz	.....	
6. Eugene Tango	.....	
7. Prog. Rosy Two Step (Spot)		
8. Maryland Blues	.....	
9. Quadrilles	.....	
10. Delilah Waltz	.....	
INTERVAL		
11. Polka	.....	
12. Blues Glide	.....	
13. Waltz Cotillion	.....	
14. La Mascotte	.....	
15. Chrysanthemum Waltz	.....	
16. Mississippi Dip	.....	
17. Veleta (Spot)	.....	
18. Donella Tango	.....	
19. Lancers	.....	
20. Moonlight Saunter	.....	
21. Ladbrooke	.....	
22. Last Waltz	.....	

Wellington Loco Horticultural Society's annual show at the Station Hotel, 1958. From left to right, back row: Charles Lewis (driver), George Fewtrell (driver), Jack Hicks (fireman), John Evason (fireman), Walter Roden (driver), Joe Burden (driver). The two judges are in the front row: on the left is Mr York from Wrockwardine; the other is unknown.

All Saints parish church members laid on a 'Bible Comes to Life' exhibition relating to Palestine, which included displays on biblical stories as well as a short play. From left to right, back row: Marjorie Swain, Jessie Shoebotham, Mrs Guthrie Clark (the vicar's wife), Mrs Leech, Mrs Titley, Mrs Leech, Mrs Heskey, -?-, Mrs Jones. Front row: John Clark, -?-, Trevor Woodward.

New Street Methodist Sunday school took regular attendees on annual treats. This group of children, parents and helpers are enjoying a day out at Drayton Manor Park in the late 1950s with teacher Elsie Price (middle row, right).

A concert at New Street Methodist church produced by Elsie Price, early 1940s. From left to right, back row: Marjorie Cotton, Ida Price, Joan Picken, Gwen Picken, Dorothy Fenn, Doreen Sumnall, Evelyn Jervis. Front row: Pat Morgan, Kathleen Hesketh, Nancy Sumnall, Margaret Fenn, ? Pritchard, Ethel Holding (bearded), Rose Titley, Margaret Morris, Peggy Price, Cynthia Whiteway, Mary Morris, Gwen Jones, Evelyn Sumnall.

Margaret Kendrick's School of Dance in a performance held around 1950. Front row, extreme left: Celia Holt. Front row, fourth from left: Celia Purcell. Front row, third from right: June Lees.

Mrs Badger's Dance School, which met at the Morris Hall off Church Street, performed in the Majestic Ballroom in the early 1950s. From left to right, back row: -?-, -?-, -?-, -?-, Johnny Knowles, -?-, -?-, -?-, Billy Firmstone, Bunny Minshall, Barry ?, George Langford. Middle row: Gloria Phillips, Pauline Mitchell, Cynthia Phillips, Shirley Lees, Gwen Cartwright, -?-, Gill Guy, -?-, Joan Twinney, -?-, -?-, Pauline Moseley, Joyce Belshaw, June Lees. Front row: Pat Guy, -?-, -?-, Daphne Holland, Carol Meredith, -?-, Gaynor Meredith, -?-, -?-, Carol Smitherman, Susan Moseley.

The Wellington branch of the Toc H society, early 1950s. William Morris stands second left, Mr Ferriday sits second left and Urban District Council chairman Cecil Lowe sits on the extreme right.

Many organisations, societies and clubs held annual dinner dances, usually during December. The Wellington and District Caledonian Society was no exception. This dinner took place at the Majestic Ballroom in 1951, when Chieftain Dr G. Pollock presided.

Children of the primary group at New Street Methodist Sunday school enjoy party games in the old church room, 1958. The teachers are, from left to right: Margaret Frost, Angela Morris, Barbara Lowndes, Audrey Magness, -?-, -?-.

Sunday School Anniversary, in the modernised New Street Methodist church c. 1958. Anniversaries such as this were appreciated by parents and friends, who came to see their children sing and recite poetry.

Father Christmas visits the Christmas party held in 1954 for the children of employees of the Chad Valley Wrekin toy works, New Street. Factory parties such as this, with games, presents, ice cream and jelly, were great fun.

Members of Wellington Youth Club, based at Constitution Hill School, enjoy a coach trip to Rhyl, 1946.

Babes in the Wood, New Street Methodist Youth Club's first attempt at staging a pantomime in the wooden Institute behind the church, 1947. From left to right: Doreen Poulter, -?-, Vera Powis(?), -?-, Norman Morris, Ann Reynolds(?), Marjorie Jones, Margaret Jones, Jean Childs. Decor for the production was created on a shoestring budget as many wartime restrictions were still in force.

Members of New Street Methodist church and friends at their 1947 Eisteddfod, during which many activities and competitions were devised for the enjoyment of young people. This event was the brainchild of Revd J. Edgar Noble (towards the back, centre), the resident minister at the time. The author's sister, Margaret, stands at the extreme right of the front row.

nine

New Street Methodist Youth Club

New Street Methodist church began a social club in the autumn of 1943 to cater for the needs of its younger members, with reduced subscriptions for forces personnel and government workers stationed in and around the town. Concert parties were arranged, as well as the opportunity to play Beetle, table tennis, darts and so on. A few church officials were opposed to what they saw as a potentially immoral and spiritually dubious enterprise but the majority of leaders voted to give the venture a try. Although they didn't know it at the time, it would lead to the creation of what was probably the most successful youth club in the town's history.

The author's aunt, Elsie Price, was not only a member of the church choir and a teacher in the Sunday school, she also had musical and organisational skills which were put to good use in the late 1930s when she produced several concert parties. These were stage entertainments put on by youngsters at the church, including her own daughter, Ida, who had a distinctive singing voice.

Elsie, with help from Ken Jones (who later became organist and choirmaster at the church) continued to produce concert parties during the war years and, in addition to making use of children's talents, embarked on performances by and for adults attending the social club. Wartime Wellington was crammed with men and women who found themselves in an unfamiliar environment away from friends and family, which made life very difficult for them. Cheap forms of evening entertainment were essential to ease the tensions and misery suffered during bleak times.

New Street Methodist church's social club began on 28 September 1943 and continued after 1945. It catered for all tastes and, as time went by, expectations and distinctive needs led to the club being divided into two separate groups in September 1947: a senior youth club specifically intended for youngsters aged between fourteen (school leaving age at the time) and twenty-five, and a junior club for children aged between seven and thirteen (one of whose leaders in the late 1950s was Harry 'Concrete' Davies, who gained his nickname by organising path-laying around the Institute buildings where the club met). Many of those attending, including the author, were regulars at the church's Sunday school, in which several of the senior youth club members were teachers. The junior club helped youngsters play together by taking part in team games.

The leader of the senior youth club was Ken Jones, who attended several courses to gain a better understanding of what a good club should offer its members. It led to association with other, national, groups who were able to advise on various matters so that the club's activities didn't stagnate. Senior members of the club formed a Youth Cabinet, which undertook to oversee disciplinary matters as well as organise events.

There were no restrictions on who was allowed to join the club. The only requirement was that every member took part in a few minutes of 'devotion' (a brief talk with a religious or moral theme followed by a hymn and a prayer) towards the close of each club night. It has been said on many occasions that this youth club was, in many ways, a marriage bureau or the equivalent of a dating agency. Yet how were teenagers from respectable families supposed to find a partner when parental control and moral values forbade the frequenting of public houses? There was precious little else to do during long evenings without incurring unacceptable expense. Even a visit to a café with a pleasant ambience wasn't possible after normal shop closing hours. One of the reasons for the success of the Methodist and other clubs at the time was that they gave the opportunity for teenage boys and girls to meet in a 'safe' environment, away from pubs and other 'bad' influences.

Older members of the church helped to run, for example, keep fit and gymnastics (Les Frost) and football (Ray Picken). Members weren't forced to take part in something which held no appeal and were content to play darts, table tennis or dance to music played on an old record player under which steel springs had been fitted to minimise the needle jumping from track to track while the wooden floor of the Institute bounced. Evening dances, called socials, soon became regular events; not only dancing but also group games like Coach and Horses and Bigamy and competitions took place. Refreshments took the form of a buffet or perhaps fish and chips from Case's in High Street, washed down with tea or coffee or fizzy drinks from O.D. Murphy's pop works on Holyhead Road.

The wartime social club had let people know that, just because a club is attached to a church, enjoyment doesn't have to rely on religious themes. Members were attracted to join and came from villages and farms in the area and from the town itself. New ideas for activities came from the members themselves as well as from the leaders. As the 1950s progressed, so did the number of people owning their own vehicles, which enabled members to visit other clubs for sporting fixtures and social gatherings, go rambling and camping in the Shropshire and Welsh hills and even canoeing on the river Severn. As an addition to normal club nights, Ken Jones and his wife, Ida, held small Fellowship gatherings at their home at Bridgend, Orleton Lane, on Sunday evenings, where discussions took place on all manner of subjects.

The club gained the envy of other clubs by being the first to take members away on holiday to the seaside during the August bank holiday week from 1951 onwards. The group usually stayed in school premises, where classrooms became dormitories for the week and beds were lilos or canvas camp beds, with grey serge (very itchy and smelling of mothballs) ex-army sleeping bags or blankets. Members saved small amounts each week to pay the £5 or so it cost for the holiday; there is no doubt that very few youngsters (let alone their parents) could afford an annual holiday. The benefits cannot be overstated. Not only was everyone supervised, transported, fed and accommodated for a whole week but they were also taken to interesting sites as well as to the seaside. Organising the holiday was never easy, especially during the early years when food and petrol rationing had to be considered, yet everyone had a great time and returned home wanting to know where the next year's holiday would be.

Whereas the holiday was strictly for club members only, an annual pantomime production was staged at the beginning of December from 1947 for the enjoyment of the general public. People came from far and wide to experience what was tantamount to a professional performance. Again using the varied talents of church as well as club members, rehearsals began in September, as did the creation of scenery and props. The latter was under the control of the author's father, Les Frost, whose home became a production warehouse for a giant's and crocodile's head (with flashing green eyes), an enormous tangerine spider, a hen that 'laid' eggs when its back was pressed, countless furry rats with tinfoil top hats ... the list was endless. If something ingenious needed to be made, he'd put all his Sankey design and draughting skills into practice. Other regular helpers were Laurie Marsh (Wellington's librarian and a talented lighting expert) and Muriel Bishop (who painted wonderful scenery). But it was the dedication of cast members that made these shows such a success; even the most unlikely candidates could be cajoled into learning lines and songs and performing to a large audience.

The 1950s was undoubtedly the most progressive and exciting period in the club's history.

Do you know that our Youth Club :-

Is run by a Youth Cabinet which is elected by the members

That there is an average membership of 46

The age limit is from 14 to 25 years

Is affiliated to the Shropshire Association of Youth Clubs, the National Association of Girls Clubs and Mixed Clubs, and the Methodist Association of Youth Clubs

Has a Football and Netball team which is in the Wrekin League

Do you know that many happy hours are spent there on Monday, Wednesday and Saturday evenings, and most of all that there is a welcome waiting there for YOU

A youth club needs to attract new members if it is to succeed. This advertisement was placed in the programme for the 1950 pantomime performed by club members. It shows a range of tempting activities then on offer. There would be many more introduced in subsequent years.

A concert party at New Street Methodist Social Club around 1943, with costumes made from blackout material. From left to right: Ted Etheridge, Elsie Price, Frank ?, Marjorie Harper, Ken Jones, Nellie Jones, Albert Rowlands, Anne Aldridge, Griff Jones, ? Rowlands. Ken Jones became leader of the subsequent youth club.

Opposite below: A club holiday boat trip on the river Dart, 1954. Ida Jones sits front row, second from left and 'Pop' Mason on the extreme right. This was one of many excursions taken during the holiday week.

Above: The first club holiday took place in cramped accommodation at Barbrook in 1951. From left to right, back row: Mr F. 'Pop' Mason (coach driver), Mrs Mason, Peter Boughey, Maureen Twinney, June Perkins, Vera ?, -?-, Sylvia Burrows, Doreen Burrows, -?-, Bob Edge, Marjorie Jones, Margaret Miles, Mary Frost, Doreen Sumnall, Ida Jones, Roy Borwitz, -?-, Ron Leeke, -?-. Front row: Gordon Fox, John Davies, Jean Childs, Graham Smith, Mabel Buttery, Laurie Cooks, Ken Jones, Joyce Cotton, Jill Mason, Mary Gale, Muriel Seabury, Pat Twinney, Margaret Jones, Peter Jones. Some members went on early morning fishing trips ... and gutted the fish afterwards for eating.

New Street Methodist Youth Club Holiday   M Gregory
July 29th to August 7th 1955.

YOUR ADDRESS WILL BE:- THE SECONDARY MODERN SCHOOL FOR GIRLS, CURLEDGE ST,
PAIGNTON.

COST £5.10.0d. THE BALANCE OF WHICH MUST BE PAID ON OR BEFORE
Plus 2/6 for breakfast on arrival & River trip
TIME OF   MON. JULY 11.

DEPARTURE:- FRIDAY JULY 29th AT 10.00P.M. FROM NEW STREET CAR PARK.

EACH MEMBER OF THE PARTY IS INSTRUCTED TO TRAVEL WITH AS LITTLE LUGGAGE AS
POSSIBLE AND WILL NOT BE ABLE TO TAKE MORE THAN ONE CASE. IT WILL BE ADVISABLE
TO TAKE SANDWICHES WITH YOU FOR THE JOURNEY, AND WE SHALL TAKE THE TEA URN.
OUR RESPONSIBILITY FOR FEEDING YOU WILL BE FROM SATURDAY LUNCH.
PLEASE TAKE WITH YOU:- MEDICAL CARD, SHEETS OR SLEEPING BAG, BLANKETS, PILLOW
AND PILLOW-SLIP, TOWELS, COAT HANGER, MIRROR & TOILET REQUISITES.
WE SHALL PROVIDE MATTRESS OR LILO TO EACH MEMBER OF THE PARTY.

YOU ARE RESPONSIBLE FOR SEEING THAT ALL YOUR BELONGINGS ARE CLEARLY MARKED.
WE SUGGEST THAT YOU WRAP YOUR BLANKETS IN STRONG BROWN PAPER AND PLACE UNDER
YOUR SEAT IN THE BUS. NOT ON THE RACK.

FIRST AID EQUIPMENT WILL BE AVAILABLE AT THE CENTRE.

THERE WILL BE CERTAIN LIGHT DUTIES TO BE PERFORMED EACH DAY AND GROUPS,
DUTY LISTS & TIME TABLES WILL BE POSTED ON THE NOTICE BOARD AT THE CENTRE.
PRAYERS WILL BE HELD EACH MORNING BEFORE BREAKFAST, AND WE HOPE THAT
ALL WILL ATTEND THE SERVICES AT THE NEAREST METHODIST CHURCH AS ON
PREVIOUS YEARS.

PLEASE TAKE GREAT CARE OF ALL PROPERTY AND EQUIPMENT, AND PLEASE
ADHERE STRICTLY TO THE TIME SCHEDULES.

FINAL INSTRUCTIONS FOR THE HOLIDAY WILL BE GIVEN AT A MEETING TO BE
HELD IN THE Room ON JULY 26th AT 7.30PM. IT IS IMPORTANT
THAT ALL SHOULD ATTEND.

Your Seat in the Bus.

			DRIVER	EMERGENCY DOOR.
DOOR			WK JONES	MRS JONES.
MRS WILEY.	MRS. MASON.		W.L FROST	" FROST
IAN DONALDSON.	D. FROST.		V. DONALDSON	D. GRINDLEY.
JEAN DAKIN.	C. ROGERS.		M. TURNER	C. MORRIS
J. DAKIN	A JONES.		M. DENN.	M. GALE.
R. ATTRILL	B. DONALDSON		M. JONES.	HILDEGARD.
M GREGORY.	D WILSON.		M MACHIN.	M. FROST.
G. JANES	K. GRIFFITHS		N. ARCHER	R. PARTON
C. GALE.	K. TURNER.	D. SHORE.	E. WAKELY	P GALE.

(marked vertically: J. WILEY)

Time Schedule.

7.30am. RISING BELL   8.15am. WARNING BELL FOR PRAYERS.
8.20am PRAYERS.   8.30am BREAKFAST.
1.00pm LUNCH.   5.00pm. TEA.
        9.30-10.30 PM SUPPER.   11.00pm LIGHTS OUT.

SPECIAL ARRANGEMENTS FOR MEALS WILL BE IN FORCE ON TOUR DAYS I.E.
TUESDAY & THURSDAY, AND YOU WILL BE NOTIFIED OF THESE.
DEPARTURE TIME FOR TOURS IS 10.00 am.

Above and opposite: Everyone going on the club holiday was expected to follow rules telling them where to sit on the coach and what their duties were, to ensure smooth running at all times.

NEW STREET METHODIST YOUTH CLUB HOLIDAY. PAIGNTON. 1955.

ORGANISING SECRETARY & TREASURER. Mr. W.K. JONES

COOKS. MESDAMES. W.K. JONES. L. FROST. F. MASON WILEY.

GROUP SUPERVISORS. MESSRS. V. DONALDSON & L. FROST

SWIMMING PARTIES ARRANGED BY Mr. L. FROST

COACH DRIVER Mr. F. MASON.

DUTY PARTIES.

1
MARJORIE JONES
HILDEGARD.
KENNETH TURNER.
PETER GALE
IAN DONALDSON

2
MARGARET FROST
ROSEMARY ATTRILL
BRIAN DONALDSON.
MICHAL MACHIN
ROGER PARTON

3
MARGARET TURNER.
CHRISTINE MORRIS.
CHARLIE GALE.
DERECK SHORE.
JIM DAKIN.

4.
JEAN DAKIN
CYNTHIA ROGERS.
GRAHAM JONES
JIM. WILEY
~~NEVILLE ARCHER~~
David Frost

5
MARGARET DEAN
MARGARET GREGORY.
DEREK WILSON.
~~David Frost~~
Neville Archer

6.
MARY GALE
EDWARD WAKELEY
ALLAN JONES
DAVID GRINDLEY.

ON ARRIVAL AT PAIGNTON, AS SOON AS IT IS CONVENIENT, **EVERYONE** IS EXPECTED TO HELP PREPARE THE DORMITORIES, MAKE BEDS, ETC **BEFORE** GOING OUT.

LIST OF DUTIES

No. 1. SETTING TABLE FOR BREAKFAST AND WASHING UP AFTERWARDS.

No. 2. SETTING TABLE FOR DINNER & WASHING UP AFTER OR PREPARING & SERVING PACKED LUNCHES.

No. 3. SETTING TABLE FOR TEA & WASHING UP AFTERWARDS.

No 4. SETTING TABLE FOR SUPPER & WASHING UP AFTERWARDS.

No. 5. PREPARING VEGETABLES — REPORT DIRECTLY AFTER BREAKFAST.

No. 6. TIDYING DORMITORIES & TOILETS — REPORT DIRECTLY AFTER BREAKFAST.

FOR DUTIES 1–4 REPORT 20 MINS BEFORE THE MEAL. **BE PUNCTUAL.**

ROSTER

DUTY No.	1	2	3	4	5	6
SAT. JULY 30	–	1	4	3	2	–
SUN. " 31	5	6	1	2	3	4
MON. AUG. 1	3	4	5	6	1	2
TUE. " 2	1	2	–	5	–	6
WED " 3	6	3	2	4	5	1
THURS " 4	3	4	–	6	–	5
FRI. " 5	2	5	6	1	4	3
SAT " 6	4	2	3	–	1	–

GROUP NUMBER

THESE DUTIES HAVE BEEN WORKED OUT AS EQUALLY AS POSSIBLE BUT CAN BE CHANGED BY ARRANGEMENT. THE SUCCESS OF THE HOLIDAY DEPENDS TO SOME EXTENT ON YOUR CO-OPERATION, YOUR CHEERFUL DISCHARGE OF THESE SMALL DUTIES AND YOUR PUNCTUALITY.

The 1959 New Street Methodist Youth Club holiday in Paignton, Devon, was a combined affair. The Wellington club was joined by Doncaster Methodist Youth Club. Reverend Maurice Hart (back row, extreme left, wearing glasses) had been minister at Wellington before taking up a similar post at Doncaster and it was at his suggestion that the joint venture was undertaken.

Club members were invited to enter floats in the annual carnival at Combe Martin, Devon. 'Sweeney Todd' and 'A Skiffle Group' (which won third prize in the comical section) were the 1957 entries. From left to right: Christine Clements, -?-, Dave Grindley, John Parton, Brian Donaldson, Graham Smith, -?-, Alan Jones, Joyce Belcher, Margaret Morris(?), Charlie Gale, Edward Wakeley, -?-.

ten

Sporting
Events

At a time when most people didn't have a television set and a limited range of programmes were broadcast on radio, pastimes and sporting activities were an important facet of life. Cinemas and dance halls, although popular, were not available every day of the week and could not always be afforded. The war had encouraged folk to do as much as possible to keep themselves occupied in the cheapest ways possible.

Minority-interest activities like crown green bowling and putting were available during summer months at the Bowring Recreation Ground off Haygate Road, which also had tennis courts and a large field in which football and cricket matches could be played by amateur clubs wishing to play friendlies against each other or more competitive fixtures between members of Wellington and District leagues. There was also a bowling club at the Charlton Arms Hotel in Church Street; bowling greens had been a feature at a few of the older drinking establishments during the nineteenth century but, by the 1940s, the one at the Charlton Arms was the sole survivor.

During the 1930s, some people from more financially secure backgrounds formed their own small-scale tennis clubs, usually making excellent use of a private court in one of their member's gardens: perhaps the best known and consistently well attended was that in Waterloo Road. Members of these clubs might also be actively involved in bridge and whist drives, where social interaction was probably more important than competitive play. Another tennis club used courts near Christ Church, off Mill Bank.

Snooker, played at the Billiards Hall in Tan Bank, was not the most favoured sporting activity at this time; snooker halls, for some reason, were regarded as unsuitable venues for impressionable teenagers in much the same way as public houses. However, public houses were not necessarily frequented by inebriates; a considerable number of them had very active darts and dominoes teams and some were able to extend their range of activities to include football and skittles.

Sporting activities were considered an essential part of school curricula, to the extent that at least one afternoon per week and at least two periods (between forty-five minutes and one hour each) were spent by pupils taking part in various physical activities. The afternoon sessions tended to be dominated by team games whereas shorter periods were filled with gymnastics and swimming. Taking part in swimming usually meant the whole class jogging to Wellington Baths, spending a short period in the water followed by a frantic run back to school (often in clothes flung over wet bodies to save time) so that pupils weren't late for their next lesson.

Team sports were, of course, seasonal, with football and rugby for boys and hockey and netball for girls dominating the autumn and winter terms (when dreaded cross-country runs were occasionally sprung on dismayed boys at the grammar school), and cricket and rounders taking place in summer months, when tennis and athletics were also enjoyed. Matches against other schools and clubs usually took place on Saturday mornings, when participants were transported to away fixtures in rickety buses. Parents seldom turned up to watch the proceedings but those that did could be seen shivering on the touchline.

However, annual school sports days featuring a variety of field and track events were well attended by parents, often to their offspring's annoyance and embarrassment. Whereas pupils at the secondary schools confined themselves to mainstream events, children at the junior schools were able to take part in more exciting trials, like sack, egg-and-spoon and slow bicycle racing.

Several older children and teenagers attended youth clubs based in Wellington and neighbouring townships and were able to extend their range of sporting activities to include table tennis, badminton, cards, darts and dominoes. Youth clubs also presented other opportunities for sport, such as canoeing, camping, hiking and mountain climbing. For a short time around 1950, competitive events between clubs attached to churches were held at Bennetts Bank Youth Centre. Children and adults alike enjoyed visiting the riding schools at stables run by Jean Worrall (behind Hollybush Farm in Golf Links Lane) or at the Park Hotel in King Street.

Although cricket was moderately popular in schools, Wellington did not have a town team until 1946. Ken Corbett from Leegomery Road was its first chairman and the Wrekin College kindly let the club use its impressive pitch for practice. Despite interest, it was difficult to raise enough players to form a regular team during the first two years. Then Col. Herbert (later Earl of Powis) of Orleton Park offered land on his estate to be used as a permanent cricket ground; it has been there ever since, with The Wrekin Hill forming an impressive backdrop to the pitch. Whereas membership increased to the extent that it became possible to field a second team, the ladies' team failed to attract sufficient regular players and only lasted for two seasons. Nevertheless, wives and partners of regular male players and officials devoted considerable time and energy providing post-match teas and helped organise whist drives and rummage sales to keep the club a welcoming place for visitors and, equally important, solvent.

The Buck's Head ground, where Wellington Town football club played semi-professional matches in front of supporters who were not as numerous as the club would have wished, occupied an important place in Wellington's sporting scene. Club officials were dominated by local businessmen who, over the years, donated regular sums from their own pockets and profits to keep the club going. It was largely because of their civic consciences and generosity that the football ground and its facilities were made available as a venue for important town events, such as the annual carnival, horse shows and similar crowd-pullers.

Annual sports day at the secondary modern school in Orleton Lane, c. 1950.
Henry Bowles, Wellington Urban District Council chairman at the time,
presents a trophy to one of the winners.

Bowring Recreation Ground, off Haygate Road, early 1950s. Crown green bowling and tennis were enjoyable pastimes near well-tended gardens. A large field catered for team sports while refreshments were available from the administration building in the centre.

New Street Methodist Junior Club outing, c. 1959. One of the more popular venues for evening trips was Carding Mill Valley, Church Stretton, where team games were an effective way to pass the time ... and tire the children out! Among the adults pictured here are club leaders and helpers Harry Davies, Neville Archer, Maggie Childs, Mary Frost, Ida Jones, Margaret Miles, Miss Picken and bus driver Ron George of George Cooper's, Oakengates. Among the children are Kevin Barlow, Gillian Bennett, Jacqui Bennett, Susan Brown, Veronica Brown, Beryl Davies, Jean Foulkes, Shirley Harris, Celia Jones, Dale Loynton, Winifred Loynton, Shirley Matthews, Gillian McCleod, Barry Oliver, Belinda Oliver, Gillian Southern, Lynn Stirling, Andrew White, John White and the author.

Senior XI football team of the secondary modern school in Orleton Lane, autumn 1955. The team includes C. Evans, J. Evans, K. Finch, M. Foulkes, F. Gater, D. Groucott, M. Handley, T. Hanke, B. Hyde, M. Morgan, D. Parry, G. Sumnall and K. Treherne.

Schools in the town made regular use of the Wellington public swimming baths. Pupils of Wrekin Road School proudly display their winners' shield, c. 1953. The teacher is Mr Rogers. From left to right, back row: Bruce Armstrong, David Turner, John Pearce(?), John Pardoe. Middle row: Charlie Lowndes, Wes(?) Fletcher, Anthony Spruce(?), Bob Groves, David Hayward. Front row: Peter Wheatley, Richard Nicholls, Roger Davies, Ron Jones, Trevor Mason, -?-, Bobby Lambert.

Boys' Grammar School First XI football team, 1954/55. From left to right, back row: Alan Villers, George Benbow, John Moule, Derek Davies, John Gough, Derek Whittingham. Front row: Paul Ramsden, Derek Tart, Alan Davies (captain), John Butler, Gilbert Band.

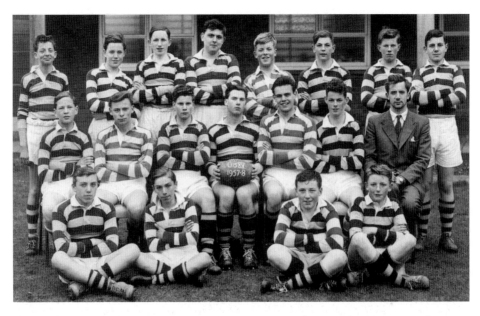

Boys' Grammar School Under-15s rugby team, 1957/58. From left to right, back row: -?-, -?-, Dave Harvey, W.C. Newbold, Norman Watterson, G. Wearing, Michael Grainger, Ralph Edwards. Middle row: N. Earle, Ian Holloway, Brian Eleanor, David Frost, Christopher Wallis, Richard Guy, Mr Clegg. Front row: S.G. Lumsden, Ron Harris, Michael Ashton, Allan ?.

Hiatt Ladies' College rounders team, 1957. From left to right, back row: Barbara Downes, Margaret Lewis, -?-, Susan Kenna, Linda Rowson. Front row: Gillian Parton, Isobel Gwynne, Margaret Beddows, Glennys Case, Judy Jones.

Girls' High School junior netball team, 1953/54. Back row, extreme left: Jane Savage. Front row, extreme left: Margaret Frost. Front row, centre: ? Griffin.

View over the cricket field, Wrekin College, *c.* 1950.

Girls' High School hockey team, 1958. From left to right, back row: Joyce Elcock, Jennifer Morris, Sheila Thomas, Marion Dolby, Pamela Small, Margaret Brown. Front row: V. Smith, Sandra Shepherd, Diana Evans, Eileen Thomas, Sheila Bardsley.

Prize winners at Park Junior School annual sports day, *c.* 1956. From left to right: -?-, -?-, -?-, -?-, house captains Gerald Rochelle and Elaine Chetwood, headteacher Ralph Brookes, -?-, Cllr Herdman, Ronnie Evans, Julian Parker, Mr Fowler (teacher).

Gymnastics display at the Girls' High School, 1948. Note the row of prefabricated changing rooms running parallel to Regent Street. This field was the site of the town's horse fairs until the mid-nineteenth century.

Above: The billiards hall inside Rechabite Hall, Tan Bank, mid-1950s.

Left: Landlord James Candlin of the Crown Inn in Crown Street (the road is named after the inn) holds a trophy in the back yard of the public house, 1940s. Rivalry between pubs competing in a variety of sporting events throughout the year gave rise to strong feelings of loyalty. Darts and dominoes were the most popular games but some pubs had sufficient numbers of regulars to enable them to field football and cricket teams in local leagues. The former inn's premises are currently occupied as offices for the popular *Wellington News* with its editor Dave Gregory.

Opposite above: Waterloo Road Tennis Club, *c.* 1945. From left to right, back row: Bill Davis, Eddie Goodyear (manager of the town's WHSmith shop), Jack Turner, John Grant, George Jones, Ivor Leonard Machin. Middle row: ? Mellor, Winnie Shelton, Nora Machin, Ruth Morris, -?-, Hilda Bowles. Front row: Michael Machin, Janet Davis.

Opposite below: Angling was another popular sport. This annual licence was issued by Mr Gorman of Wrekin Rose Nursery, off Haygate Road. Fishing licences were issued by Walter Davies in Walker Street after Mr Gorman died, and by Wheeler's pet shop in New Street from the early 1950s.

No. 16219

SALMON AND FRESHWATER FISHERIES ACT, 1923.

SEVERN FISHERY DISTRICT

SEVERN FISHERIES PROVISIONAL ORDER, 1911.
SEVERN DISTRICT FISHERY ORDER, 1926.
FRESHWATER FISHERIES (SEVERN FISHERY DISTRICT) ORDER, 1943.

1944

License to Fish with **Single Rod and Line** for Freshwater Fish

(Not Transferable).   Not available after the 31st December, 1944.

Mr. _____ of _____

_____ in the County of _____

having paid the sum of TWO SHILLINGS AND SIXPENCE for this License, is hereby authorised to fish for FRESHWATER FISH with a SINGLE ROD and LINE, at the times and places at which he is otherwise entitled so to fish, within the whole of the Severn Fishery District.

    Given under the Seal of the Board of Conservators   H. LLEWELLYN JONES

of the Severn Fishery District this_____   CLERK TO THE BOARD

day of _____ 1944 at ____   a.m.   25, THE TYTHING,
                                         p.m.   WORCESTER

(Signed) **W. C. GERMAN** ....Distributor.

FISHING TACKLE SPECIALIST,
IRONMONGER & SEEDSMAN,
Brook, Highley, near Kidderminster.   N   ROSE HURST,
Teme and tributaries above Tenbury Wells   WELLINGTON.
Bridge.

BOARD OF SEVERN FISHERY DISTRICT CONSERVATORS

CLOSE SEASONS.

TROUT. Severn and tributaries above Borle
Brook, Highley, near Kidderminster. } 1st Sept.
Teme and tributaries above Tenbury Wells } 1st March.
Bridge.

Severn and tributaries below Borle Brook, } 1st Oct.
Highley, near Kidderminster. } to
Teme and tributaries below Tenbury Wells } 1st April.
Bridge.

OTHER FRESHWATER FISH } 15th March
Throughout the District. } to 15th June.

ALL DATES ARE INCLUSIVE.

SIZE LIMITS.

TROUT AND GRAYLING. All waters above the junction }
of the Severn and Vyrnwy. } 7 inches
Severn and tributaries above Ludlow Bridge. }
Any other part of District. } 9 inches

BREAM, ROACH, DACE, PERCH AND CHUB. Through- }
out the District except the Severn and tributaries } 7 inches
above the junction of Severn and Vyrnwy, and the }
Teme and tributaries above Stamford Bridge. }

GUDGEON. Throughout the District except the Severn }
and tributaries above the junction of Severn and } 4 inches
Vyrnwy, and the Teme and tributaries above Stam- }
ford Bridge.

There is no size limit in the excepted areas for freshwater fish other than trout.

Trailing or trolling with natural or artificial spinning baits from boats in motion is prohibited.
Contests are only allowed in waters rented or owned by the Board with the Board's written permit.
No person is allowed to fish in the Board Water during a Contest other than anglers taking part in Contest.
This license does not give permission to the holder to fish any water other than that rented or owned by the Board unless the consent of the owner has been obtained.
The use of Keep Nets for undersized fish is prohibited. Bank or Hand Lines are illegal.
This license must be produced on demand to any Water Bailiff, Honorary Water Bailiff or Constable, and to any other licensee on producing his own license.

N.B.—Will anglers kindly notify any pollution immediately it is observed. Cost of call or wire refunded.

Before 5 p.m.
Worcester 4682

After 5 p.m.
Worcester 4047

Tommy Nicholls, once member of Wellington Youth Club at Constitution Hill and the Amateur Boxing Club at Sankey's, realised a dream in the Olympic Games held at Melbourne in 1956 when he won a silver medal. During his boxing career, he became national Amateur Boxing Association bantamweight champion (the first of four titles from the Association) in 1950 while serving in the RAF, won the Imperial Services Boxing Association crown, the European Championship belt at Berlin in 1955, and over thirty international vests. In 1956, while in Moscow, the Russian press called him 'The Master of the Gloves'. He decided against becoming a professional boxer.

New Street Methodist Youth Club girls' football team, formed on holiday as a one-off to play against a local team at Combe Martin, Devon, 1957. From left to right, back row: June Stokes, Shirley Smith, Margaret Gregory, Joyce Belcher, Valerie Picken, Margaret Morris, Christine Clements. Front row: Marion Sumnall, Carol Smith, June Smith, Barbara Lysons. The team lost 1-7 but managed to raise £20 for carnival funds.

Above: New Street Methodist Youth Club girls' team, Inter Church Sports, seen here at Bennett's Bank County Youth Centre, early 1950s. From left to right, back row: -?-, Mabel Buttery. Front row: Doreen Sumnall, -?-, Lianna Chetwood, Nancy Sumnall, Margaret Jones. *Below:* The boys' team. From left to right, back row: Derrick Jones, Peter Jones, Graham Smith, John Talbot, Norman Morris. Front row: Ken Hughes, Dennis Burrows, Don Weston, Dennis Rowley, ? Poole.

Wellington and District League

Division I

	P.	W.	L.	D.	F.	A.	P.
Stirchley United ...	12	8	3	1	31	17	17
Wrockwardine Utd.	9	8	1	0	34	12	16
Oakengates Y. C. ...	10	6	1	3	36	21	15
Hadley C. W.	12	5	4	3	23	29	13
Much Wenlock T. ...	7	3	0	4	17	8	10
Shifnal Juniors	8	4	2	2	24	15	10
Wellington Rovers ...	10	4	4	2	27	23	10
Allied United	7	4	1	2	20	18	10
Tibberton	12	4	7	1	29	29	9
Wellington Town 'A'	9	3	4	2	23	22	8
Old Wellingtonians ..	10	4	6	0	23	35	8
Albrighton United ...	10	3	6	1	18	26	7
Madeley Miners ...	12	2	9	1	21	54	5
Broseley Athletic ..,	12	1	11	0	24	43	2

Results: Albrighton Utd. 2, Tibberton 1;
Madeley Miners 0, Shifnal J. 4; Stirchley
Utd. 5, Broseley Athletic 1.

Division II

	P.	W.	L.	D.	F.	A.	P.
Hinkshay United ...	12	11	1	0	84	14	22
St. George's J. A. C.	9	8	0	1	50	15	17
Roden	11	7	3	1	38	22	15
Ketley United	12	7	4	1	41	32	15
Ketley Bank	10	6	2	2	51	16	14
New St. Methodists	10	6	2	2	33	22	14
New Dale United ...	13	4	7	2	34	51	10
Newport Town Res.	8	4	3	1	24	21	9
Oakengates Y. C. ...	10	3	6	1	20	21	7
Hadley Y. C.	13	2	9	2	24	75	6
Lilleshall Institute ...	7	1	3	3	15	19	5
Iron-Bridge Y. C. ...	6	0	6	0	7	24	0
British R. S.	9	0	9	0	12	78	0

Result: Roden 1, Hinkshay United 2.
Challenge Cup.—Round I: Newport Tn.
Res. 0, St. George's J.A.C. 9; Oakengates
Y. C. 2, Ketley Bank 5.

Above: Methodist Youth Club football team, Wellington league, 1953. From left to right, back row: Peter Jones, Bill Lee, Ron Hicks, Ted Rawlinson, John Lucas, Alf Burrows, -?- (referee). Front row: Dave Brown, Ken Roberts, ? Edwards, Tom Farmer, Ron Poulter.

Left: Wellington and District football league placings, November 1952. So many young men were keen to play that almost every village and township, as well as several factories and schools in the area, was able to field a team on a regular basis. Football was by far the most popular team sport in post-war years.

Opposite: The cover of a Wellington Town Football Club programme from April 1955, with the club's achievements given prominence at the top of the page. Most club officials were businessmen in the town.

WELLINGTON TOWN FOOTBALL CLUB

CHESHIRE LEAGUE CHAMPIONS 1945-46, 1946-47, 1951-52
WELSH SENIOR CUP WINNERS 1901-2, 1905-6, 1939-40
CHESHIRE LEAGUE RUNNERS-UP 1952-53

PRESIDENT : E. W. JONES, ESQ.

CHAIRMAN : F. NAGINGTON, ESQ.

VICE-CHAIRMAN : T. G. PEARCE, ESQ.

HON. TREASURER : MR. P. BRISBOURNE

COMMITTEE :

MESSRS. E. A. AUSTIN, T. G. AUSTIN, R. BURTON, P. D. DICKEN,
R. LATHAM, W. MANSELL, W. PROUSE, S. J. L. ROBERTS, H. G. STONE

SECRETARY : MR. O. L. SAXTON

TEAM MANAGER: MR. G. ANTONIO

OFFICE AND GROUND :
WATLING STREET, WELLINGTON
TELEPHONE 332

OFFICIAL PROGRAMME THREEPENCE

663

After the Match

Pay a visit to the

Robin Hood Restaurant

Near Bus Terminus and Railway Station

Also Sherwood Cafe, Tan Bank

LUNCHEONS - TEAS - SUPPERS

Parties specially catered for at short notice

FREE CAR PARK

Telephone   -   -   166

WE ARE AT YOUR SERVICE

for

Printing of every description

John Jones & Son

King Street, Wellington

Estimates Free   **Phone 126**

★ All your catering requirements attended to by . . .

WHEELER
& SONS

NEW ST., WELLINGTON
and Dawley

After the match visit our . .

FISH AND CHIP PARLOUR
We are specialists in hospitality

HOBSON & Co.

(STATIONERS) LTD.

Printers and Manufacturing
Stationers

Picture Framers and
Fancy Goods Dealers

MARKET SQUARE

Phone :   Wellington 54

For Fountain Pens, Ball Pens, etc.

T. & E. Austin

The Newsagents

45   HIGH   STREET

and

19   CHURCH   STREET

WELLINGTON

also at

44 High Street, Hadley

Phone: Wellington 245

For all your

Agricultural Seeds and
Fertiliser   Requirements

Ed. Turner
& Son Ltd.

Agricultural
Merchants

WELLINGTON

Some advertisements from Wellington Town Football Club programmes during the early 1950s, all relating to businesses which no longer exist. Advertisements such as these paid for the programmes to be produced and printed by John Jones of Church Street (he later moved to King Street).

Wellington Journal & Shrewsbury News photograph of Wellington Town Football Club, 1945/46. From left to right, back row: J.L. Rigby, Heber Onions, Harold Bates, ? Merrington, A. Ferrington, ? Bates, ? Lea, T. Barnett, ? Jones, T. Brothwood, Bert Richards (trainer), E. Austin. Middle row: L. Saxton (secretary), J.T. Stone (chairman), H.F. Hodgson (president), R.W. Jones (vice-chairman), G. Pearce (treasurer). Front row: ? Phillips, ? Saxon, ? Simms, ? Driscoll, ? Cross, ? Childs, H. Chaplin.

eleven

Schools

The 1940s witnessed a substantial increase in the number of schools in Wellington. In the years leading up to the Second World War, the government made vast sums of funding available for the building of new schools throughout the country. In Wellington, this led to the creation in 1940 of a new grammar school for boys on former farmland off Golf Links Lane: the existing High School premises in King Street, which served both boys and girls, had become too small for the increasing numbers of pupils.

Constitution Hill, Princes Street and Wrekin Road Schools had also become overcrowded and a new, mixed-sex, secondary modern school was built off Orleton Lane, also in 1940. But the problem of insufficient accommodation continued, partly because of an increasing child population (known throughout the country as the Baby Boom which covered the war years through to the 1950s) and partly because of the development of new housing estates. Consequently, additional primary schools opened at Barn Farm and Orleton Lane, and St Patrick's Catholic schoolchildren found themselves in new premises in North Road after leaving their old school on Mill Bank, which had been the town's Catholic church until the present one in King Street, adjacent to All Saints parish church, opened in 1906.

Social developments and changing attitudes affected private schools in the town. Some, like Hiatt Ladies' College in King Street and The Grove School off Whitchurch Road did not survive into the 1960s. Old Hall School on Holyhead Road was one which would continue to flourish (at least for the time being). Only the Wrekin College could be considered as having a strong and guaranteed future. The war affected the structure of society in many ways and the middle classes, who had traditionally sent their children to private schools, found their income did not stretch quite so far as it had prior to 1939. Furthermore, standards of education in state schools, with new examination systems and generally better facilities, had made them an attractive (and affordable) option.

School uniforms helped create a unifying spirit of belonging ... and helped identify miscreants who misbehaved in public. From an early age, children were taught by rote and were encouraged to do mental arithmetic and spelling exercises. The subject range was limited by modern standards yet there were very few pupils who did not benefit from these methods. By the mid-1950s, some relaxation had crept into the way teachers communicated with their classes but not to the point where respect for the teaching profession encroached on behaviour or standards.

Sports were strongly encouraged. Matches and competitions between local, county and regional schools were frequent; the Wrekin Area Sports, for example, gave aspiring athletes a chance to compete against their peers. Cultural activities were also an important feature: orchestras, operettas, plays and even fashion shows gave a practical aspect to learning. Religion played an important role in morning assemblies as well as providing opportunities for annual performances of nativity plays in churches as well as schools.

Sunday schools thrived during the period; it wasn't until the 1960s that irresistible alternatives and new forms of entertainment chipped away at what was, for many folk, an important day of the week, a day when 'Sunday best' was worn, the family gathered around to eat Sunday dinner after attending a church service together and no shops (apart from newsagent's and the duty chemist) were open for business.

Opposite below: All Saints parish church garden party held at Wrekin College, July 1953. From left to right: Revd Cresswell, Revd Bourne, Gordon Cook, Revd Makepeace, Mrs Cecil Lowe, Revd Maurice Hart (New Street Methodist church minister), Cecil Lowe, Mr Millichap, Revd Whild(?).

Above: Wrekin College, *c.* 1950. The college started life as Wellington College in April 1880 at No. 33 Albert Road, home of John Bayley. It changed its name to Wrekin College in January 1921 to avoid confusion with Wellington College in Berkshire.

Wrekin College science building, *c.* 1950.

Wrekin College gardens in the 1940s.

Opposite below: The 'babies' class at Hiatt Ladies' College, *c.* 1948. From left to right: Jill Pascall, Judy Fray, Veronica Whittles, -?-, Miss Reeves(?), Susan Davidson, Margaret Cresswell(?), Jennifer Beaton, Judy Bale, Jennifer Roberts, -?-.

Above: The Hiatt Ladies' College playing fields off Albert Road in the late 1940s, with Constitution Hill School in the background. These grounds formerly belonged to Sunfield School.

Above: Girls' High School, King Street, 1959. Until 1940, when the Boys' Grammar School opened, both boys and girls had been educated here. It later became a sixth form college for the town and is now New College.

Members of the Girls' High School orchestra at a rehearsal during the 1950s.

Girls at the High School enrol in the Red Cross, June 1950.

Opposite below: Headmistress Miss Ethel Barnes sits with prefects of the Girls' High School during the 1951/52 academic year.

Pupils at the Girls' High School presented Gilbert and Sullivan's *The Mikado* in 1951.

A performance of George Bernard Shaw's *Androcles and the Lion* by the Girls' High School, March 1959, produced by Kath Robinson and S.E. Evans. Among those taking part were Sheila Bardsley, Pauline Brayne, Juliet Brookes, Inez Cadman, Lois Clark, Wendy Clifford, Di Davis, Hilary Downes, Andrea Evans, Diana Evans, Lilian Greenfield (the lion), Lorna Grice, Janet Hawkins, Brenda Jones, Janet Meeson, Jennifer Morris, Pauline Morris, Rosalind Morton, Sue Pointon, Marion Rawson, Richardson, Susan Shakeshaft, Anne Shaw, Pamela Small, Carolyn Sockett, Jacqui Stordy, Jennifer Swift, Eileen Thomas, Sheila Thomas, Jaqueline Wakeley, Pauline Whittingham, Patricia Wynn Green. The (unseen) bugler was Patricia Young.

The Girls' High School staged nativity plays at New Street Methodist church in 1956 (*above*) and All Saints parish church in 1949 (*below*).

Wellington Grammar School for Boys was opened in 1940, built on land off Golf Links Lane which had previously been farmland. The specially designed Art Room, with high windows sloping into the roof, can be seen on the right. The Ercall Hill, part of which was used for the school's cross-country course, is visible in the background.

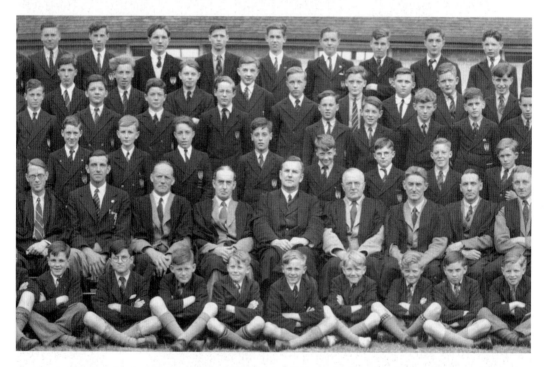

An extract from a school photograph taken at the Boys' Grammar School, June 1950. The masters in the second row are, from left to right: Arkinstall, Hassall, Hanby, Martin (deputy head), J.P. Thorpe (headmaster), Marshall, Tomlinson, Wellings, Parry-Jones.

Opposite below: The Boys' Grammar School orchestra in the main quadrangle at the school, early 1950s. John Butler sits with his cello on the extreme right of the front row. The music teacher was Mr Knighton.

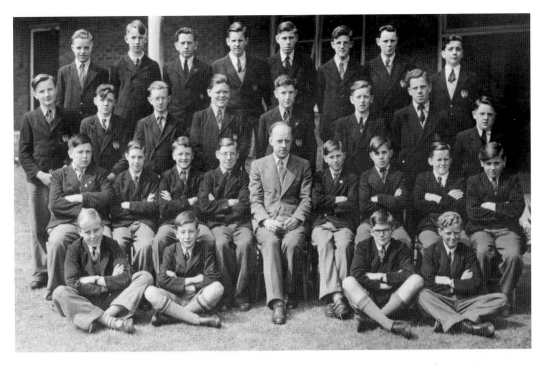

Above: In addition to full-school photographs, individual form photographs were taken. This one is of Mr Hamilton's class in 1951/52. From left to right, back row: Hancox, Hamer, Phillips, Thompson, Hayward, Vickers, Gilmore, Clayton. Third row: Padmore, Edwards, Stagg, Butler, Beechey, James, Mitchell, Simpson. Second row: Gough, Band, Owen, Beeston, Mr Hamilton, Boycott, Barnes, Price, Edwards. Front row: Hames, Harrison, Worrall, Yapp.

✓	Dunn. Making animal noises in library	R.K.
✓	Ferrington Bullying	I.RE
✓	Dunn Fighting in ~~the~~ Cloakroom	D.R.
✓	Langley C.R. Insolence & disobedience	A.R.J.
	~~Grant~~	~~P.H~~
✓	Price D.H. No lines	cP.
✓	Jones M.H. No lines	cP.
✓	Haywood A.J Banging door in face of other boys	cP.
✓	Talbot. Insolence	G.I.H.
✓	Talbot Disobedience	G.I.H.
✓	Dean	
✓	Downes Attempting to deceive	M.A.C.
✓	Langley c.l Rank Disobedience	RGH
✓	Garvey 'Being nosey.'	RGH
✓	TALBOT. failure to do penance.	RGH.
✓	Ogden No lines	D.R.
	Jones .B.D. Gross Insolence in Library.	P.E.M.
✓	Ogden, Failure to hand in Lines	P.E.M.

Left: Extract from the grammar school captain's Penance Book. Disobedient pupils (with their offences entered in its pages by a prefect) were obliged to suffer detention after normal school hours; a tick signifies detention was served.

Below: Boys at the grammar school stage a performance of Shakespeare's *Macbeth* during March 1956.

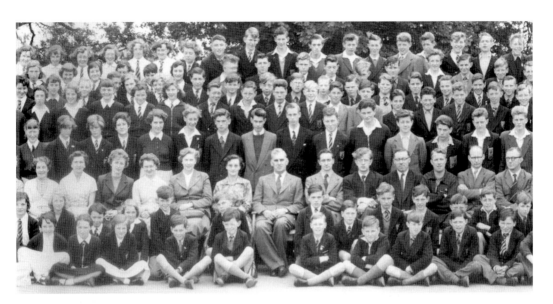

Above: Extract from a photograph of the secondary modern school, 1958, with headmaster Alfred Shimeld in the centre of the second row.

Right: Schools with playing fields needed someone dedicated to look after them. Bill Ward was groundsman at Orleton Park Secondary Modern School in the 1940s.

One of the events staged by pupils attending the secondary modern school in the mid-1950s.

The Finding of the King nativity play performed by the secondary modern school in 1951, directed by Miss E. Watson. The chief characters were Marion Brocklesby (angel), Albert Archer (innkeeper), Tony Cotton (vagabond), Anne Small (Gaspar), Sylvia Bythell (Melchior), Doris Yale (Balthazar), Wilfred Jones, Graham Price and Peter Galloway (shepherds), David Picken (Roman soldier), Brita Taube (Mary). Music, under the direction of and composed by R. Broome, was rendered by the school orchestra, pipe band and choir.

The top year at Wrekin Road Junior School, 1953. From left to right, back row: David Inions, Martin Williams, John Cotton, Lionel Llewellyn, Glyn Jones, Graham Cudd. Fourth row: Nigel Griffiths, David Frost, Hugh Keats, Richard Guy, Ross McFarland, David Osborne, Frank Picken, Gordon Love, Michael Gaut, Douglas Hudson. Third row: Pauline Whittingham, Evelyn Giles, Brenda Forsythe, Joan Hughie, Susan Savage, Denzil Brisborne, Bridgit Bone, Ann Owen, Betty Edwards, Joyce Elcocks, Vera Barber, Diane ?. Second row: Helen ?, Heather Dabbs, Diane Boughey, Sheila Bardsley, Catherine Dean, Marlene East, ? Reynolds/Richards(?). Front row: Graham Pritchard, Leon Shears, Richard Nicholls, Roger Davies, Nigel (Henry) Johnson, Roger Dixon, Peter Wheatley.

Opposite below: Some 180 children enjoy a Christmas party at the newly opened Orleton Lane Primary School, 1951. Father Christmas gave each child a gift; those not able to attend were sent a present and a parcel containing 'Christmas fare'.

A class of children attending Constitution Hill School, 1947.

Princes Street School, senior class, *c.* 1949. The author's sister, Margaret, is in the front row, third from left.

twelve

Scene
Changes

Wellington underwent considerable change during the 1940s and 1950s. The war affected the whole structure of society in countless ways. Ordinary folk began to question their role in post-war Britain and local councils began to exercise their new-found powers (particularly in respect of town planning) with a vengeance.

There were, of course, many benefits to be enjoyed by the town's inhabitants yet, as has been the result of powers invested in or seized by the present-day Borough of Telford and Wrekin, a scant regard for the area's historic buildings led, inevitably and ultimately, to a diminution of the traditional (largely Victorian) character of the area. This period saw the beginning of a long and destructive process which, once started, could not be reversed. Many of Wellington's buildings would disappear or have their outward appearance changed beyond recognition.

UPON INSTRUCTIONS FROM THE EXORS. OF E. GROOM, ESQ., DEC'D.

Of particular interest to Farmers, Developers, Speculators, Builders,
Hotel Keepers and Others.

SHROPSHIRE

The widely known

FINE FREEHOLD ESTATE

within half a mile of the Market Square of

WELLINGTON

DOTHILL PARK

The whole enclosed and walled (6 ft.) in a perfect ring fence, and occupying a unique and most valuable situation, with over a mile of Valuable Frontage to the main Whitchurch and Admaston roads ; with a total extent of slightly under

200 Acres

Superb Property for Occupation as a

RESIDENTIAL FREEHOLD FARM

and Small Sporting Estate, with unlimited scope in the greater part for

HOUSING AND RESIDENTIAL DEVELOPMENT.

The Estate is at present occupied as a productive

MIXED DAIRY AND ARABLE FARM

with Georgian Residence, Picturesque Grounds and Gardens, ample Buildings, Four Cottages, Fishing Pools and Small Lake, Highly Productive Pasture and Arable Lands, with full Sporting and Residential Amenities.

Affording wide scope for excellent occupation in numerous spheres :
FARMING, DEVELOPMENT, HOTEL, ETC., ETC.,

and to be offered with

IMMEDIATE VACANT POSSESSION

Upon Completion of the Purchase, and to be sold in ONE or THREE LOTS (Lot 1 : A Residential Farm of 121 acres ; Lots 2 and 3 : Valuable Accommodation Building Land of 42 and 33 acres) and which, subject to Conditions,

BARBER & SON, F.A.I.

will submit to Auction

At THE CHARLTON ARMS HOTEL, WELLINGTON,

On THURSDAY, 12th OCTOBER, - at 3 p.m.

Detailed Particulars and Plan from the Solicitors : FOWLER, LANGLEY & WRIGHT, Wolverhampton (Tel. 20261) ; or from the Auctioneers' Offices, Wellington (Tel. 27 and 444), and at Stafford and Market Drayton.

The eastern segment of All Saints parish churchyard in 1952, shortly before its conversion into a tidy and well-maintained Garden of Rest. A few intact old headstones were propped up against the wall adjoining the Catholic church; the rest were used for paving.

Interior of All Saints parish church, 1940s.

Opposite page: Following the death of Edward Groom of R. Groom & Sons, the medieval estate at Dothill was offered for sale in 1944. It enabled the development of a vast housing estate, complete with schools, in the north-west of the town.

Another property to be demolished for housing development: Park Walls, offered for sale in 1943.

Number 15 Bridge Road, once a tasteful private residence, was put up for sale in 1952. It became the offices of accountants S.C. Parker & Co. Many larger residences in Wellington have undergone a change of use from domestic to business premises.

An aerial view from the early 1940s, showing the Girls' High School (centre left) in King Street. Part of the playing fields had been commandeered by the council to create allotments during the war (bottom left) and included an air-raid shelter. Other allotments can be seen alongside New Church Road (centre right), named after Christ Church (top centre).

Examples of recently constructed conventional brick-and-tile and modern prefabricated council housing seen from the rear of Montgomery Road, looking towards The Wrekin Hill. Precast concrete bungalows made by the Lilleshall Co. were cheap to construct and were a marked contrast to the slums in which their inhabitants had lived before the Second World War. This area was known by many as 'the back of the gasworks' council estate and came with some misguided views that its residents were somehow inferior. The fact that one of the town's former rubbish dumps had been located in this area seemed to endorse that opinion. Wellington Urban District Council recognised the importance of providing each home with a small garden, although the road system through the estate did not anticipate that, in time, many of the inhabitants would own cars. However, planners did understand that streets with bends (like Clift Crescent) were more imaginative than traditional straight ones (such as Walker Street), a few of which had been laid out during the Middle Ages.

Left: 1947 produced a particularly harsh winter. Kevin Hitchin clears the path outside his home in what was then the top of New Street, with now-demolished properties in High Street to the right.

Below: Cecil Herring pauses to chat to a shopper. The Ansells sign outside the Three Crowns public house can be seen on the right. On the far side of the road, Frost's bakery wall is to the left of Ivy Dickin's greengrocery, while notorious Kipp's Cafe and Tranter's surgical boot making workshop jut out into the road further to the right. These properties also no longer exist.

Opposite below: Christmas auction at Wellington Smithfield, 1955. The original Smithfield began 100 years earlier and moved to Bridge Road on 23 March 1868. Its closure in January 1989 had a devastating effect on the town's trade.

Above: Buckatree Hall, once the home of Sir John Bayley, founder of Wrekin College, was sold in 1943. It became a hotel in 1960 after being purchased by John Wilson of the Swan Hotel, Watling Street.

Other local titles published by Tempus

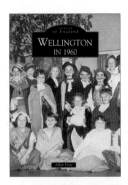

Wellington in 1960
ALLAN FROST

Wellington was a thriving market town in 1960, serving the needs of neighbouring farming and industrial communities as well as its own inhabitants. This collection of archive photographs of the town is a unique snapshot of Wellington in the days when it held a position of historical and social importance in east Shropshire. *Wellington in 1960* is a nostalgic look at how the townspeople lived, worked and played at that time.

0 7524 2630 3

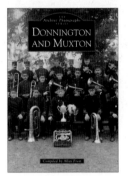

Donnington and Muxton
ALLAN FROST

Long before the development of Telford, there was a Royal Forest with numerous small villages, including Donnington and Muxton. This fascinating history covers the development of this area from the Dark Ages to modern times and is illustrated with archive photographs, diagrams and maps. The social history of the area is also examined, with chapters on local religious activities and schools.

0 7524 2250 2

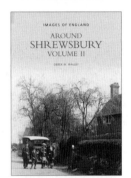

Around Shrewsbury Volume II
DEREK M. WALLEY

This collection of 200 archive pictures highlights some of the developments that have taken place in the county town of Shrewsbury during the last century. Important events are recalled, including a visit by King George V in 1914, alongside aspects of everyday life, from schools and churches to shops and local industry. Life in some of the surrounding villages is also remembered, including Acton Burnell, Dorrington, Longnor, Baschurch and Shawbury.

0 7524 3371 7

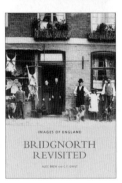

Bridgnorth Revisited
ALEC BREW

This absorbing collection of over 200 archive pictures highlights the developments that have taken place in the Shropshire market town of Bridgnorth during the last century. Every aspect of life in Bridgnorth is explored, from schools, churches and shops to sporting achievements, ceremonies and events. One chapter documents the history of RAF Bridgnorth and the history of some of the surrounding villages is also recalled, including Worfield, Burwarton and Ackleton.

0 7524 3637 6

If you are interested in purchasing other books published by Tempus, or in case you have difficulty finding any Tempus books in your local bookshop, you can also place orders directly through our website

www.tempus-publishing.com